Serving Boys through Readers' Advisory

Michael Sullivan

American Library Association
Chicago   2010

Michael Sullivan is the author of *Connecting Boys with Books* (American Library Association, 2003), *Fundamentals of Children's Services* (American Library Association, 2005), *Connecting Boys with Books 2: Closing the Reading Gap* (American Library Association, 2009), the Escapade Johnson series of children's books, and the juvenile fantasy *The Sapphire Knight* (PublishingWorks, 2009). He has spoken widely on the topics of boys and reading, library administration, and the future of public libraries. He is currently an adjunct faculty member at Simmons College Graduate School of Library and Information Science in Boston, Massachusetts. He has won a U.S. Conference of Mayors City Livability Award and the Mom's Choice Award for juvenile fiction, and he was the 1998 New Hampshire Librarian of the Year. Sullivan earned his master's degree in library and information science from Simmons College.

While extensive effort has gone into ensuring the reliability of information appearing in this book, the publisher makes no warranty, express or implied, on the accuracy or reliability of the information, and does not assume and hereby disclaims any liability to any person for any loss or damage caused by errors or omissions in this publication.

The paper used in this publication meets the minimum requirements of American National Standard for Information Sciences—Permanence of Paper for Printed Library Materials, ANSI Z39.48-1992. ⊚

Library of Congress Cataloging-in-Publication Data

Sullivan, Michael, 1967 Aug. 30–
  Serving boys through readers' advisory / Michael Sullivan.
    p.   cm. — (ALA readers' advisory series)
  Includes bibliographical references and index.
  ISBN 978-0-8389-1022-1 (alk. paper)
    1. Boys—Books and reading—United States. 2. Teenage boys—Books and reading—United States. 3. Reading—Sex differences—United States. 4. Readers' advisory services—United States. I. Title.
  Z1039.B67S86 2010
  028.5'5—dc22   2009026841

ISBN-13: 978-0-8389-1022-1

Printed in the United States of America

14 13 12 11 10   5 4 3 2 1

Serving Boys through Readers' Advisory

ALA READERS' ADVISORY SERIES

The Readers' Advisory Guide to Graphic Novels

The Readers' Advisory Guide to Genre Fiction,
second edition

Research-Based Readers' Advisory

The Readers' Advisory Guide to Nonfiction

Serving Teens through Readers' Advisory

The Horror Readers' Advisory:
The Librarian's Guide to Vampires, Killer Tomatoes,
and Haunted Houses

The Science Fiction and Fantasy Readers' Advisory:
The Librarian's Guide to Cyborgs, Aliens, and Sorcerers

The Mystery Readers' Advisory:
The Librarian's Clues to Murder and Mayhem

The Romance Readers' Advisory:
The Librarian's Guide to Love in the Stacks

The Short Story Readers' Advisory: A Guide to the Best

CONTENTS

INTRODUCTION

"Don't panic!"

These are the words emblazoned on the fictional guidebook *The Hitch-hiker's Guide to the Galaxy* in the science fiction classic of the same name by Douglas Adams (Harmony, 1989). They are fitting words to put here, at the beginning of a book on readers' advisory for boys. Let's face it, boys can be a strange species sometimes, even to those of us who work with them well and on a regular basis. And boys and books may seem at times to be oil and water; the two just do not mix. The prospect of serving boys this way really is in making three connections: between boys and adults, between boys and books, and between adults and the books that speak to boys. Each of these can be a difficult connection to make. Don't panic.

On top of all that, we have to face the fact that boys are not a mono-lithic beast. They differ as much from each other as they do from girls, or librarians, or sixteenth-century armchairs. Just when you think you have a boy pegged, just when you are sure he is reading and happy with his reading, he puts down his book, climbs on the back of a sofa, gives a Tarzan yell, and leaps off into some unknown fate. Don't panic.

Do you believe in the power of reading? Do you honestly and com-pletely believe that reading is necessary, not only to be effective in this world in a financial and productive sense but to become the best person you can be emotionally, intellectually, and spiritually? Do you feel a drive to share that power with every child you can possibly reach? If the answers are all yes, then don't panic; you are going to be effective. This book is just going to give you the tools to be as effective as possible when working with boys. If the answers are all no, consider finding another line of work; this will be awfully hard without a firm motivational base.

I've worked with boys for more than twenty years now, as a teacher, coach, librarian, storyteller, and program director. They are a challenging, energetic, interesting, and diverse bunch. They can also be destructive, random, frustrating, and inscrutable as individuals. That is just fine. Be ready, be aware, and remember all those principles I just spoke of.

At the end of this book you will find a number of tools to use, so keep this book close at hand. You will find lists of great authors for boys in the various genres that I will write about. You will find lists of more than five hundred books, mostly recent, in the past five years, but also some older books that have gained recent new life. You will find a "Read-Alikes" chapter to give you books to follow up the ones that boys just loved, but also a chapter called "If Your First Thought Is . . . ," a list of books to give to boys in place of books they did not like or would not read. You will also find more than one hundred tried-and-true booktalks, little commercials to use to sell books to boys. These tools are far from complete; no one reader can cover the span of children's literature, and I am sure there will be books missing that you are sure appeal to many boys. But these are works that I have encountered and used to reach boys, and I believe they will help you as well.

I've spent most of my adult life with boys' literature, as a teacher, reader, librarian, reviewer, and author. It is a wild ride. It mirrors all the extremes of the boys who it so well serves. And it shares a common trait with those boys as well. Neither boys nor their literature are well understood, so neither gets the respect it deserves. This book will try to change that. Don't panic.

CHAPTER 1

WHY BOYS ARE DIFFERENT

It may seem strange to have a book specifically directed at readers' advisory for boys. After all, how different can it be from readers' advisory for girls? Sure, the books that you offer them may be quite a bit different, and their attitudes toward reading are likely to be skewed, and their relationship to you as the readers' advisor will involve issues most unlike your relationship to girls . . . All right, so it is not strange at all that we have a book specifically directed at readers' advisory for boys. The same can be said of why readers' advisory for children differs from readers' advisory for adults or why readers' advisory for teens would differ from readers' advisory for children. In all cases, there are basic differences not just in what the populations read but in how they read, in why they read, in how they relate to reading and those who help them read, and in how we must promote reading to them if we hope to be effective.

The most basic difference between boys and girls as readers is that the average boy does not read as much or as well as the average girl. The gap is a year and a half, on average, in reading level throughout the school years.[1] That gap starts small in the early school years but continues to grow until students reach the eleventh grade, and there is a three-year gap between the proficiency of the average boy and the average girl.[2] Sadly, research shows that the gender gap in reading is increasing.[3]

Boys' lack of success in reading is intimately tied to their lack of practice. Studies in both England and the United States confirm that the average fifteen-year-old boy reads about 2.3 hours per week, and when asked how much they read, half of American high school boys, and a third of the young men who enter the University of California at Los Angeles, identify themselves as nonreaders.[4] The first difference between readers' advisory for girls and for boys is that boys, on average, just need it more.

FLEXIBILITY

Boys will need more flexibility in readers' advisory, both in the reading level of the books you promote and in the types of books. The reading gap is largely caused by a delay in brain development; girls' brains start their rapid growth earlier than boys' brains do, and boys are behind in brain development through much of their teenage years.[5] Although boys' brains will eventually catch up, the brain lag is a reality we must remember when working with school-age kids. Reading standards, such as grade-level reading and Lexile levels, do not take the brain lag into account; they work on the assumption that a fifth-grader is a fifth-grader, and an eleven-year-old is an eleven-year-old. This simply is not true. There are a thousand reasons why one child is on a different developmental level than another child, and gender is one of the most powerful. So, boys will often be given books significantly too hard for them based on their age alone. Although at times we must help boys find books at a required level (see chapter 4, "Special Circumstances"), at other times we need to be helping boys find books that are at or even below their natural reading levels to make reading a more enjoyable experience.

You will have to promote a broader range of books to appeal to boys as well. The types of reading most often identified as the best reading, and thus most often promoted by educators, tend to appeal more to girls than to boys. This is not surprising, because the majority of teachers and librarians are female. Although no generalization will describe all kids, it is clear that very many boys, and especially the boys who are resistant or reluctant readers, will prefer nonfiction to fiction, and genres such as gothic horror, humor, and fantasy to the standard juvenile novel. (See chapter 2, "What Is Boys' Lit?")

PHYSICALITY

Boys tend to be more physical in nature than girls. A difference in brain structure makes them more likely to require stimuli, both from external sources and from their own kinetic energy, to spark brain function at its highest levels.[6] This is going to affect what boys read, as they may seek out books about the physical activities that mean so much to them. It will also affect how boys read, as they will be less likely to sit still for long periods of extended reading. Many boys will then respond better to shorter works or to works that are well divided for shorter periods of reading. This should also affect how we promote reading to boys, making us use our tools of reading promotion to differentiate reading from the solitary, sedentary activity that most boys see as reading. If we promote books about active subjects that focus on plot elements over characterization, if we promote books that are shorter and full of action, and if we promote reading through stimuli-rich activities that involve and engage boys, then we will have acknowledged the physical nature of boys.

DIFFERENT WORLDVIEWS

Girls tend to be internal thinkers, looking within themselves for a reflection of the world around them. They feel connected to the larger world, and they will feel that connections are the way to get things done. They will tend to believe that the world operates on interpersonal cooperation and communication, and they will read to understand these connections and how to use them.

Boys will tend to be external thinkers, looking outside themselves to see a world that must be explored and experienced.[7] They do not tend to feel connected to the world, and although they may crave connection, their view of the world will tend to be more impersonal. They will see the world operating on dispassionate rules. They will believe that they must understand the world and how to manipulate it if they wish to succeed. They will therefore read to understand, to categorize, and to explore.

ROLE MODELING

Boys see the world of reading as foreign, because nearly all of the people who teach them about reading, and most of the people they see reading, are female. Everybody wants to see and follow someone who looks like them. We take strong social clues from the people around us, and how much more when our worldview highlights exploration and observation? Men need to know that their presence in the reading life of boys is vital, and women need to recognize that they have this extra hurdle to clear when they try to reach boys. How to circumvent this challenge? By consciously presenting reading in ways that appeal to boys and by speaking directly to their needs.

CONCLUSION

When you look at all the differences between so many boys and so many girls, it is not surprising at all that we as educators need to address reading differently when it comes to the genders. Not all boys act in the way we would typically—some would argue stereotypically—see as "boy behavior," but enough will to make it worthwhile to keep gender in mind when performing readers' advisory. The differences we must keep in mind range from literary tastes to psychological outlook to physical distinctions. It is the whole boy that we must address, because all of him is involved in his reading. Do not pass on any opportunity to turn a boy into a reader.

NOTES

1. Donna Lester Taylor, "'Not Just Boring Stories': Reconsidering the Gender Gap for Boys," *Journal of Adolescent and Adult Literacy* (December/January, 2005): 292.
2. Lanning Taliaferro, "Education Gender Gap Leaving Boys Behind," *The Journal News* (June 17, 2001): 17.
3. Lucille Renwick, "What's the Buzz?" *Instructor* (August 2001): 8.
4. Adi Bloom, "Girls Go for Little Women but Boys Prefer Lara," *Times Educational Supplement* (March 15, 2002): 18; Steven J. Ingles, et al., *A Profile of the American Sophomore in 2002: Initial Results from the Base Year of the Education Longitudinal Study of 2002* (Washington, DC: National Center for Education Statistics, 2005), 75; Patrick Jones and Dawn Cartwright Fiorelli, "Overcoming the Obstacle Course: Teenage Boys and Reading," *Teacher Librarian* (February 2003): 9; and Christina Hoff Sommers, *The War against Boys* (New York: Simon and Schuster, 2000), 164.
5. Amanda Ripley, "Who Says a Woman Can't Be Einstein?" *Time* (March 7, 2005): 55.
6. Carla Hannaford, *Smart Moves: Why Learning Is Not All in Your Head* (Arlington, VA: Great Ocean Publishers, 1995), 80.
7. Eva M. Pomerantz, Ellen Rydell Altermatt, and Jill L. Saxon, "Making the Grade but Feeling Distressed: Gender Differences in Academic Performance and Internal Distress," *Journal of Educational Psychology* (June 2002): 396.

CHAPTER 2

WHAT IS BOYS' LIT?

Is there a type of literature that will appeal to all boys? Of course not. Each individual will have his own tastes and preferences, which is why the readers' advisory interview is so important (see chapter 3, "The Readers' Advisory Interview"). But being familiar with the types of literature with broad boy appeal is certain to help you help them. Unfortunately, many adults, and even educators, are completely unfamiliar with these types of books. It will be worthwhile to familiarize yourself with these books; you may even find them more engaging than you expect. Sure, there will be the occasional bodily function humor, but you will find quicker moving plots, shorter works, great humor, and high action, as well as themes of heroism and sacrifice. Boys' literature can be the cure for the common read.

When we talk about boys' literature, we mean the types of reading that will tend to appeal to the vast number of boys. Not every type of writing that I will deem as boys' literature will appeal to every boy, and there will be many boys who will enjoy types of reading that do not fall into this category. My attempt is to create a general guide, a starting point for those who would try to connect boys with reading. Indeed, there are types of reading that experience shows have broad appeal among boys. It is vital that we take these generalities as instructive, not normative. The hope is that we can use these generalities as tools for connecting kids with books. The fear should be that by identifying a type of literature with maleness, we stigmatize boys who have other tastes and outlooks as being inappropriate and feminized. The goal is to make it clear that all tastes in reading are honored; excessive zeal can produce the opposite result if we are not vigilant. That said, and although we should always try to understand the particular viewpoint of every reader, this discussion may point us in a general direction.

There are types of literature that will appeal to many boys, and so when turning to the bookshelves, it may be useful to have some types of literature in mind as good starting points. It may well be that the bookshelves themselves are not the right starting point. After all, the idea is to connect boys with reading, not necessarily books. Boys read more material outside the traditional book format—what we would call nonlinear reading—than girls do. Nonlinear reading means text that does not flow continuously for the length of a book and might include magazines, newspapers, web pages, and comic books.[1] Though we may know these things intuitively, we do not always have these considerations foremost in our minds when we recommend reading to kids.

Many boys connect with what we would call periodical literature, magazines and newspapers. The writing in these venues often involves short passages with immediate, practical application. Mostly, boys read periodical literature because that is what they see men read. A 1996 study asked kids which parent reads more books; respondents named their mothers ten times more often than their fathers. When they were asked which parent read more newspapers, their answers were reversed, and the children pointed toward their fathers ten times more often than their mothers.[2] Also, boys seem to be more sensitive to the currency of the things they read. Newspapers and magazines are more up-to-date than books or any other reading boys are likely to encounter, short of online texts.

Online reading is increasingly becoming a part of boys' reading, and again, some of that is apparently because boys often imitate the reading habits of men. A *BusinessWeek* study in 2005 showed men were reading fewer magazines and doing more of their reading online, including online magazines: "Men aren't migrating so much from the content of magazines as from the format."[3] Those who work with boys, and who understand that boys' reading often mirrors men's reading, would do well to keep track of this trend. Indeed, many types of reading that boys value, such as digital reading, are often overlooked by adults such as teachers, parents, and librarians.[4] We often miss the reading lives of boys because they often do not read books. We lose a great opportunity by not honoring nonbook reading.

That being said, readers' advisory ultimately does come down to putting the right book in a child's hands. But what constitutes the "right" book? Part of the answer to that question is in understanding the reader, which will be looked at in chapter 3, "The Readers' Advisory Interview." Part of the answer lies in the circumstances of the quest, many of which will be explored in chapter 4, "Special Circumstances." The rest of the answer is in the books themselves, and this we will address here.

DEFINING BOYS' LITERATURE

How do we describe boys' literature as a whole? What are the traits that make a book boy-friendly? None of these are universal, meaning that not every book with boy appeal will have all of these elements, but it is fair to say that they must have at least some of them. Of course, it helps to have boys as the main characters; everybody likes to read about people who are like themselves. Boys will often prefer books written by male authors. This represents both a need for role modeling, the nearly universal tendency to look for those who share key traits, and a particular confidence issue for boy readers. Much of the literature pushed on boys does not in fact represent the types of books those boys enjoy. Many of our boys feel disconnected from reading because they have been given reading that does not speak to them for most of their reading lives. There is a belief among many boys that a male author may at least share their point of view. Right or wrong, fair or unfair, this belief may affect how boys choose books and how they see the reading we offer them.

There is also a long tradition of boys, even preadolescent boys, turning to adult authors. This runs in the face of other truisms, that boys on average read at lower levels than their female counterparts and that reading below your natural reading level makes you a better and more confident reader. The tendency toward adult writers is a legacy of the time when there really was little literature available with high boy appeal, and even less was being promoted by educators. Boys who were being presented with little to their liking in children's literature went quickly to the adult literature that spoke to them, when they were allowed to do so, that is. This tradition should be honored by the readers' advisor of today. There are many adult authors who write books that could spark the interest of adolescent and preadolescent boys.

Boy books will focus on plot elements—the action and progression of the story—over characterization and character development. Boys are more likely to be outward thinkers, so the books should focus outward to the greater world and less inward toward personal feelings and relationships. Yes, we bemoan the fact that boys do not get in touch with their feelings enough, but every book does not need to be the way the boy gets in touch with his inner self. And boy books need not be devoid of introspection; it just should not be the dominant perspective of the book.

Books for boys often highlight the fun of reading over the challenge of reading. Jon Scieszka, author of the Time Warp Trio series, has seemed to find the winning formula. The characters in his books tend to be two to three years older than the reading level of the book. These are not dumbed-down books, or what we traditionally call the "high/low" readers (high interest level, low reading level); they just are books with simpler, more straightforward sentence structure. They avoid complicated imagery and use clear, direct language to tell a story. Many authors, including myself, have taken this example to heart when writing books aimed at boys.

Clear and direct writing not only makes books easier to read but it makes books seem more real to boys. So when defining boy books, you can see that they focus less on description, imagery, metaphor, and other devices that make a book a mystery. One researcher, while addressing one type of literature, spoke for males and reading in a broader sense, "To some men, more comfortable with the literal and the explicit, it seems that both poems and women expect you to read between the lines. What teachers see as subtlety or implication sometimes gets translated in boys' minds into a blind hunt for secret messages and the perverse notion that literature has hidden meanings. What kind of nutty person would try to hide meaning? Why can't they just come out and tell you what they mean?"[5]

The other part of highlighting fun over challenge is this: boy books tend to be short. Part of the fun of reading for a boy is the sense of accomplishment. They want to finish the book. They want to tell you how many books they finished. They want to reach the end. If you think of boys' literature as plot based, then a story line is a meaningful unit. The best contemporary example of this comes from Gordon Korman, a great boy writer who really understands the adolescent and preadolescent boy. When he wrote his adventure series Everest, Dive, and Island, he broke each of these three adventures into three distinct parts. He could have published each adventure in a big, epic tome. Instead, each adventure is presented in three separate books.

We are clearly in an era that fights this concept. Juvenile fiction titles aimed at kids as young as third or fourth grade routinely run eight hundred pages to a book. But if a boy does not read as well as his classmates, if he reads only 2.3 hours per week, and if he reads in short stretches between bursts of activity, then he is unlikely to stick with a book that long. There is nothing wrong with reading eight one-hundred-page books as opposed to one eight-hundred-page book, and the boys will like it a great deal more.

Boys' literature will also tend toward the extremes, the edgy, in both subject matter and tone. Humor is not enough sometimes to make a boy book; it has to be riotous, gross, or borderline antisocial. A book about bugs may not be enough; it must have large-scale, full-color, close-up pictures of slavering mandibles. Gore, frightening scenes, disgusting visuals—all these show up too often in boys' literature for many adults' comfort. Boys are outwardly focused. They are intellectual explorers. They want to reach the edges. Why do boys so often want to find the limits of their parents' tolerance? For the same reason explorers climbed Mount Everest: to see where it ends. This is disturbing, threatening to adults, and so nearly universal that it must be seen as perfectly normal.

THE TYPES OF BOYS' LITERATURE

When we talk about boys' literature, we must first think of nonfiction. Teachers, librarians, and parents often see a boy with a nonfiction book in hand and respond with, "That's fine; now get a book you can read." I visited a school recently to offer training on boys and reading and found its brand-new library divided into two sections, each with a large, carved wooden sign. One wing was labeled "Nonfiction." The other was labeled "Reading Books." But boys often see nonfiction not as a vehicle for finding specific information but as a way to better understand the world around them, a way of acquiring the understanding of the world around them that they so desire and believe will help them to succeed. In short, they read nonfiction the way we expect children to read fiction.

Boys often see men reading nonfiction, and this must influence their own reading habits. Men so often read newspapers and magazines, history, or whatever is necessary for their work. But from the earliest ages when children can read on their own, even as young as five or six years old, boys gravitate more toward nonfiction. Who has not seen a young child leaving his public library with arms full of truck books or dinosaur books? Thus, although male role modeling may reinforce nonfiction reading among boys, the preference begins even before adults have had a chance to mold their book-choosing habits.[6]

Ray Doiron, of the University of Prince Edward Island, observed ten thousand free-reading choices made by children in grades one through six from their classroom libraries. Boys in his study chose three nonfiction books for every four fiction books, despite the fact that more than 85 percent of the books in the libraries themselves were fiction.[7] On the positive side, studies have shown that nonfiction reading is more likely to prepare the reader for social and financial success.[8] The downside is that nonfiction, often nonlinear, is less effective in producing the kinds of social benefits, including language and communication skills, than the more narrative-based fiction texts. Still, if boys will read nonfiction in volume, the question of efficiency becomes moot.

Many nonfiction books also give boys back an important part of their reading that they lost early in their school years: illustrations. Pictures can be a powerful stimulant to a boy's brain, and because of differences in brain structure, boys benefit from stimuli in their environment when doing upper-level thinking, such as reading.[9]

We will have more and more opportunities to promote nonfiction as classrooms adjust to new pressures, requiring them to increase literacy within the subject areas. Thomas N. Turner wrote that elementary social-studies teachers can only hope to keep their places in elementary schools if they can put themselves in the literacy mix, and that to do so, all they need to give up "is their obsession with textbooks."[10] What a great opportunity to bring the library, and the librarian, into the classroom in a meaningful way, promoting books that marry the curriculum to literacy.

When they do read fiction, boys will often gravitate beyond the standard juvenile novel to the various genres. The genres often focus more on plot elements than the standard juvenile novel will. Novels tend to be more character based. Students are given a steady diet of novels in their school assignments, but they get little exposure to the genres. When doing readers' advisory, especially when helping boys find books for pleasure reading or free-reading assignments, it is worth exploring their interests in these areas.

Humor is a powerful tool for reaching boys, especially those who read below grade level or who have had problems with reading. If a child feels stressed about his reading abilities, or is feeling outwardly produced pressure, then reading humor can be a welcome relief. The child may respond to some of the more edgy humor, pushing back against the constriction of adults by seeking release in the forbidden. The fact that adults may disapprove of their choices is a plus, and the more unlike their school reading the books are, the better.

Science fiction and fantasy touch on mythological themes of good and evil and the heroic quest. These books will often rely heavily on action to push the plot forward. The more action there is, the longer many boys will spend with the text. It is often believed that boys prefer shorter texts, but many of the books in these traditionally boy-friendly genres are extremely long. Why the contradiction? Because boys who reject longer texts usually do so as a reaction to long descriptive passages or large amounts of introspection. If the plot moves fast enough, boys will stick with it.

Action and adventure stories have long been associated with boy readers. The basic form of this story is the outdoor, or nature, adventures, for which we have much to thank Jack London. The struggle of man against nature, which really comes down to man against his own weaknesses, have broad boy appeal but speak most directly to boys entering adolescence and facing their own coming-of-age.

Action and adventure books are often set against the backdrop of war, and these go back at least to James Fenimore Cooper. Here the struggle is against an identifiable enemy, not the impersonal and unyielding force of nature. We do not always think of these as action and adventure stories, because they often fall under the heading of historical fiction, but historical fiction is almost too broad a term to be used in day-to-day readers' advisory. It encompasses books that use historical realities as plot elements as well as books that simply use the historical setting as an exotic backdrop. The ones that integrate the setting into the plot will tend to be more adventurous and thus have more boy appeal.

Like action and adventure books, sports books do well among boys, and for some of the same reasons. First, they have plots that sustain the interest of the reader, making them seem less like work than novels about personal relationships do. Secondly, in their limited experience, boys see sports and adventure as things identifiably male. In these stories, boys hope to find clues to their own futures. Sports may seem like a poor metaphor for life to many educators, but many boys will feel otherwise.

Gothic horror is a genre that appeals to many boys, but it is rejected by almost as many parents and educators. Like fantasy, gothic horror deals with mythological concepts of good and evil, and in each case, there is a world with different rules that either exists apart from our world or somehow comes in contact with it. So what separates these two genres? Fantasy tends to deal with the heroic battle on the side of good. Gothic horror tends to focus on the nature of evil. Although fantasy is often highly physical and action oriented, it does not usually have the brutality or violence inherent in much horror. When the other world of gothic horror meets our world, it often threatens to overwhelm us and destroy the world that we know. These aspects make gothic horror a difficult genre to accept for many adults. But for many boys, set on understanding their world and pushing the edges of their experience, it is a more powerful conceptualization. Indeed, fantasy readers will often move into the world of gothic horror as they seek to widen their reading experience.

Some formats and genres seem to have broad appeal across genders, though not all books within these groupings will have strong boy appeal. Visual storytelling, once limited to comic books and a mostly male audience, has grown with the influence of Japanese forms to reach a broad spectrum of adolescents and preadolescents. Manga, which is serialized Japanese graphic storytelling, began as a primarily girls' format in Japan, but it has a strong male following in America and seems to have a special appeal to many boys who do not read up to the level of their age peers.

Mystery is a genre that can appeal to anyone; there are many types of mysteries, though, and some types have far more boy appeal than others. Again, the dividing line is often between those works that focus more on plot and those that focus more on characterization. The same can be said for historical fiction, as mentioned above. Some books within these genres are great ins for boys; others represent just the kind of reading many boys avoid like the plague.

Of course, many books will not fall neatly into one category or the other, and the melding of forms can create real opportunities to reach boys with books. Sports biographies combine the appeals of sports books and nonfiction. They are both real and action oriented, and they portray men doing things boys recognize as masculine. In recent times, there have been many attempts to meld humor with the prototypical boy forms of fantasy, science fiction, and horror, the last creating what I call "gothic humor."

CONCLUSION

Boys' literature covers a great deal more territory than it is often given credit for. It is not a simple dumbing down of literature. The fact that we define boys' literature out of our conception of "good" literature probably has more to do with our own outlook than the books themselves. Most educators are women, and they tend to enjoy the books that speak to them. We all must remind ourselves that there are different points of view out there, and the fact that we do not enjoy a book is not necessarily a reflection of the book's quality.

With this broad spectrum of reading, both book and nonbook reading, fiction and nonfiction, novels and the genres, children's and adult literature, you should now have the tools to face any reading need. Now the challenge is to understand the boys with whom you will connect this reading.

NOTES

1. See Alleen Pace Nielsen, "It's Deja Vu All Over Again!" *School Library Journal* (March 2001): 49–50; Susan Ashby, "Reading Doesn't Have to Damage Your Street Cred," *Youth Studies Australia* (March 1998): 46; and Deborah Langerman, "Books and Boys: Gender Preferences and Book Selection," *School Library Journal* (March 1990): 132–36.
2. Donald D. Pottorff, Deborah Phelps-Zientarski, and Michelle E. Skovera, "Gender Perceptions of Elementary and Middle School Students about Literacy at Home and School," *Journal of Research and Development in Education* (Summer 1996): 211.
3. Jon Fine, "Where the Boys Aren't," *BusinessWeek* (November 7, 2005): 24.
4. Kathy Sanford, Heather Blair, and Raymond Chodzinski, "A Conversation about Boys and Literacy," *Teaching and Learning* (Spring 2007): 5.
5. B. Pirie, *Teenage Boys and High School English* (Portsmouth, NH: Heinemann, 2002), 82.
6. Deborah Langerman, "Books and Boys: Gender Preferences and Book Selection," *School Library Journal* (March 1990): 134.
7. Ray Doiron, "Boy Books, Girl Books," *Teacher Librarian* (February 2003): 14.
8. Debbie Abilock, "Sex in the Library: How Gender Differences Should Affect Practices and Programs," *Emergency Librarian* (May/June 1997): 17.
9. Carla Hannaford, *Smart Moves: Why Learning Is Not All in Your Head* (Arlington, VA: Great Ocean Publishers, 1995), 80.
10. Thomas N. Turner, "Book Talks: Generating Interest in Good Reading," *Social Education* (May/June 2005): 195.

CHAPTER 3

THE READERS' ADVISORY INTERVIEW

Although we must always work to improve our familiarity with literature, that is not the most important part of readers' advisory. Our most important task is not to understand the reading but to understand the reader. Although this will inherently test our communication skills, every layer of difference between us and the reader makes the task just that much more difficult. For the majority of librarians, dealing with a boy reader means overcoming some gender differences, and for all librarians, this means overcoming the age differences.

And let me state this as strongly as possible: these differences always exist. It is dangerous to think that just because a child acts mature that his perspectives will be similar to yours. It is equally perilous to think that just because a boy displays few or none of the stereotypical "boy" behaviors that you can see eye to eye with him. The behaviors you encounter may have as much to do with your own perspective and what the boy thinks you want to see as they do with what is going on inside the boy's head. Indeed, it is dangerous to make any assumptions about a reader's state of mind when approaching a readers' advisory opportunity. That is why we do a readers' advisory interview.

Many of the principles behind a good readers' advisory interview are similar to those behind a good reference interview. First and foremost, the ideal is to get the customer talking. The more he talks, the more information you have with which to work. You should try to get the customer talking about what he wants, what he needs, and what is acceptable. To accomplish this, you should begin an interview with open-ended questions, meaning questions that elicit more than a short, factual answer. The problem with closed-ended questions is that they limit the possible responses, often excluding by definition the best answer. Yes or no, this or that, and either and or may not really apply. It also limits the range of information to the aspects the readers' advisor thinks are important or, more likely, those aspects the readers' advisor has thought of.

A quick example comes from my earliest days as a public librarian. An elementary-age girl came into the library and asked me for the biggest book in the library. Flustered, I asked her if by biggest she meant the most important or the longest book in the library.

"No," she replied. My either/or options were rejected.

Was there any type of book she wanted?

"No." Good intentions, but that was still a yes or no question.

Was she interested in large illustrations?

"No."

This went on for some time until, prodded by her insistence that she just wanted the biggest book in the library, I showed her the *World Book Encyclopedia*. She picked up volume *A* and looked at me doubtfully. I realized she meant the biggest volume, and I showed her the *Columbia Encyclopedia* instead. She looked thrilled and asked if she could check it out. I told her that, no, reference books cannot be taken out, and her face fell again.

You may have guessed the outcome by now, but it took me a while to finally ask the obvious open-ended question: what do you want to do with this book? "Press flowers," was her response.

It is easy to see where I went wrong and why. By asking closed-ended questions, I limited her possible responses to the uses that I would expect for the book, and her intended use of the book was beyond this limitation. This is worth remembering as we look at all the things we want to know about the readers' advisory request: the most important information may not be what we expect, so we must listen more than we talk.

WHAT WE NEED TO KNOW

What do we need to know? The traditional first two questions we ask a child who asks for a book are "What was the last book you read and enjoyed?" and "What grade are you in?" Both questions have their uses, but both are limiting in their own way. The first question takes for granted that the boy is a reader or that the boy is expecting to enjoy the reading he is about to do. These can be dangerous assumptions whenever you work with children but with boys especially. Experience tells me that a significant number of boys will answer that they have never read a book, or if they have, they never enjoyed one. Rather than getting this specific right away, it is best to get a boy talking about his reading life. Even if his response is a litany of all the reasons he hates to read, you will learn a great deal.

The "What grade are you in?" question, or the attendant "How old are you?" question, is meant to help you determine what level the boy is reading at, but this has its own perils. Boys read, on average, a year and a half below girls throughout their school years, with a small gap from the first day of school and the widest gap later on. Grade-level reading becomes more meaningless as children age. Research also suggests that reading level has little to do with a child's enjoyment of reading or the good that the reading will do for him. Children can become better readers even while reading well below their abilities, and children will enjoy texts well above their abilities if their interest level is high enough.

Both of these approaches have their uses but do not deserve the prominent place we tend to give them in a readers' advisory interview. Get the boys talking instead about what their interests are, and let them tell you whether reading is among them. Boys are more likely to connect their reading lives with their nonreading lives. Boys will tend to read to understand the world around them. With many boys, the first connection we need to make is between the boy and the plot of the book, and to do this we need to know what activities interest him. We are better at connecting readers with characters who will speak to them. This is an important part of what makes a child connect with a book, but it is likely to be more important to girls. Your first concern with most boys is to connect the reader to a plot.

If reading is one of the activities the boy identifies among his favorites, you now have the opportunity to ask what books he has read and enjoyed without alienating or shaming him. Even now, though, it is easy to categorize a boy as an enthusiastic and literary reader. The situation is not nearly so clear and simple. Reach this point often enough, and you will encounter a boy who launches into a list of all the books he did *not* like. A boy who discovers the joy of reading may still be more interested in the benefits of reading and be less enamored of the experience. That is fine; he is talking about reading, and he is making it easier for you to help him.

Whether the boy is talking about books he likes or dislikes, the key thing you need to know is why. Too often, we ask a child what he likes to read and then try to give him a clone of that book, and we end up giving him a book that matches the title he mentioned in an aspect that means nothing to the boy. The great example comes from the Harry Potter books, by J. K. Rowling. We watched so many children connect with eight-hundred-page books, and we were desperate to keep the momentum going. So authors wrote, publishers published, and educators pushed huge titles, either thinking the size of the books would not daunt readers or that readers wanted to get lost in the language and description of huge, epic tales. Clearly, some do, but as a readers' advisor, you must recognize that there are many aspects of a book that might appeal, and you have to sort out which ones affect an individual reader. Many boys who read less than their peers may gravitate to a book for one factor, even if it is a minor one, because they are unaware of other books that share that characteristic.

In the case of Harry Potter, for many boys this was their first exposure to fantasy. Granted, the Harry Potter books were as much about school stories, mystery, or even romance as they were fantasies, but for younger boys who had been steered away from fantasy, the fantasy elements of the books were a revelation. For those boys, the most effective next book might be something more classically fantasy, such as *The Amulet of Samarkand*, by Jonathan Stroud (Miramax, 2003), from the Bartimaeus Trilogy series, rather than one of the more modern fantasy series or even a coming-of-age, school-based novel.

As an author, I face this all the time. While attending a book group for one of my books, *Escapade Johnson and Mayhem at Mount Moosilauke* (PublishingWorks, 2006), at a middle school, I listened as the moderator asked the kids what they liked about the book. I would have considered the book primarily humor, but the students all chorused that what appealed to them was the action. The moderator then asked what they didn't like about the book. One boy pointed at the open book and said, "Nothing happened on this page." These boys, and it was an all-boy reading group, connected with an aspect of the book that I, as the author, would not have dreamed would be so important to them. Seriously, one of them actually noticed, and remembered, a page with no significant plot motion. What chance does a readers' advisor have to recognize such an obsession? A great chance, actually, if we learn to listen without the filter of preconception.

Letting a boy talk about what he liked and disliked about a book he read also allows you to see if there is some type of book that he has not read that he might like to try. Again, the less reading a boy has done, the less he might know about his options. I am amazed at how many boys who hate reading complain that it is just a bunch of "dumb stories" and "make believe." From the early years of elementary school on, many boys are told, either explicitly or implicitly, that nonfiction does not count as reading. We believe that children read nonfiction to find information, but many boys approach it to find understanding and place themselves in the world. In effect, many boys read nonfiction the way we would expect children to read fiction, if they are given permission and encouragement to read nonfiction at all.

Boys may complain that the books they read are too long, and what they really mean is that they cannot sit long enough to make progress through them. These boys may be completely unaware of the various types of visual literature, including graphic novels, manga, and highly illustrated nonfiction works for older kids. Worse, they may have been told, directly or indirectly, that these types of reading do not "count." Such visual fiction stimulates the brain and cuts down on the active behaviors that boys often engage in to stimulate brain function and that is often simply dismissed as short attention spans.

One piece of information you must have to be effective with boys is where the impetus for the readers' advisory question comes from. Did the boy decide he wanted to find a book, or did someone decide for him? If the latter, then who and why? This is true for any readers' advisory with children, but especially so with boys, whose reaction to outside-dictated reading is likely to be more negative than with many girls. The most likely outside motivation for a readers' advisory question would be teachers or parents. Is the request because of a homework assignment? Is there a parent behind the request, worried about the boy's reading and trying to jump-start it? These issues make for a very different readers' advisory experience and will be dealt with in chapter 4, "Special Circumstances."

WHAT WE DO *NOT* NEED TO DO

Those special circumstances aside, the request then becomes one for pleasure reading. Pleasure reading is widely acknowledged as the best way to develop as a reader and to gain the habit of reading as a lifelong activity. Boys seeking pleasure reading do not need to be judged on their reading. That is true for anybody, but so much more so for boys, whose reading is often denigrated and even dismissed. Whatever your opinions about what constitutes "good" reading, whatever you hope children gain from their reading, you have to allow for the fact that you are not a twelve-year-old boy, and your views may have precious little to do with what actually will appeal to the boy before you. Remember that it is reading in volume that makes a good reader, not reading a certain type of book.

Likewise, it is not the level of reading that makes reading valuable, but the volume. Children's librarians are more likely to interact with better readers on a regular basis, and they should always be aware that they may overestimate the ability of a child based on his age. If the boy does not identify a reading level that he prefers, do not presume to be able to judge that level. Boys may benefit from reading material well below their abilities, both from a developmental as well as a psychological perspective. Lower-level reading often translates into a greater volume of reading. Lower-level reading may also be a stress response, or a stress release. Boys read, on average, a year and a half below their female counterparts throughout the school years, and they hear about it. Many boys feel a great deal of pressure to read "at level," even though grade-level reading is an arbitrary distinction that does not take into account differences in brain development. Many boys respond to this pressure by choosing books of a type, like humor, or at a level that relieves the stress.

Conversely, some boys will gravitate to reading seemingly far above their abilities. This poses an even greater challenge to the readers' advisor who truly wants to help boys become involved and excited readers. We fear that reading that is too hard will discourage boys, and the only reason they want to pick up that huge, advanced tome is because of some social pressure. So we have invented techniques to test children's abilities and discourage them from choosing books that are too hard. One of the most common is the five-finger rule. We ask the child to read a page and count on his fingers words that he does not understand. When he reaches the fifth finger, the book is too hard, and he should choose something else.

Although the intention here is admirable, the practice is ineffective. First, if he is indeed daunted by the level of reading, he will put the book down and is not likely to be scarred for life by the experience. We have all put down books that do not resonate with us; boys will do the same. Second, interest will almost always trump ability. If a boy is motivated enough by the subject, he might very well find a way to read enough of the text to get what he wants from it. And if there is social pressure behind the choice, what of it? Reading as a social activity is bound to be more effective than reading as an isolating activity. Do we not practice this principle with our "One Community, One Book" programs? Peer pressure is a neutral concept; we should use the positive kind whenever we can.

Ultimately, the best approach is to offer the boy a number of reading levels and not try to limit him to his grade-level reading, or his natural reading level, for that matter. Encourage a boy who is looking for a good book to take home three and choose the one, or two, that he enjoys the most.

ISSUES OF POPULARITY AND QUALITY

Ultimately, the question of the type of book, and even the difficulty of a book, comes down to the tension between popularity and quality. We believe in the power of reading to transform, and we want the greatest transformation possible from the reading experience. We may even fear the power of reading to transform in a negative way. Good books are good books for a reason; they change people for the better. On the other hand, we want the reader to feel the same joy at the experience of reading that we do, and we want them to come back for more. Popular books are popular for a reason; people enjoy reading them.

We may be looking to stretch the reader to engage with a book that, by some standard, is better, has a stronger impact, or is likely to produce more lasting value. Such distinctions are both difficult and perilous; they are always at least partly based on personal views, or if you like, personal prejudices. Still, many teachers and librarians are trained to make such distinctions, they have a wealth of experience at making these distinctions and the wisdom that comes from both successes and failures, and people expect them to make such distinctions. In fact, if people did not trust our judgment in such matters, then they would not come to us for readers' advisory at all.

If we have an impulse to apply a filter of our own perception of quality when recommending reading, how much stronger will that impulse be when working with children, for whom we feel an extra sense of responsibility as guides to their reading? How much stronger even when working with boys, who we know do not get enough exposure to reading? If boys indeed read less than girls do, and significantly less than we adults want them to, then do they not need our greatest vigilance against reading that is merely enjoyable?

As a readers' advisor, you should make an effort to recognize these impulses when they come to mind, and recognize that, as admirable as they may be, they may be inwardly focused where the focus should be on what the reader wants. When the boy asked for a suggestion, did he express a desire to improve the quality of his reading, or his life? Did he mean he wanted a book of high quality, a book that is appropriate by some standard, or one that he will enjoy for the pure exercise of reading it? If their goal is enjoyment, or utilitarian value, then it is a disservice to impose our view of quality over their needs. And if quality really is the goal, did he define quality from his own perspective? Usually not, so you should get him talking again about what he means by a "good book."

If we are concerned about the quality of the books we put in a boy's hands, then we need to get some perspective on the idea of quality. What is a "good" book? If it seems Clintonian, if it seems that quality is well and universally defined in literature, consider the places where quality literature for children is found: awards lists and school literature curriculums. Now go back and look at the types of literature that tend to appeal to boys. You will find very little overlap. Gothic horror books will be nearly invisible, and sports books do not often win the Newbery Medal. When we teach language in schools, we act as if we are preparing all our students to be novelists, yet most will read and write nonfiction exclusively for their jobs.

Are humor writers just worse at writing than authors who write about family tragedies? Are action and adventure stories inherently less well written than stories about psychological struggles? Or are boys simply less discriminating than girls when it comes to reading? I do not believe any of these are the case. We have, over long years, anointed certain types of reading as superior. The fact that these types of reading tend to be the ones that, on average, speak more to girls than to boys probably reflects a lack of understanding about differences in outlook between boys and those who choose the best literature, many of whom are women and almost all of whom happen to be adults. Books that appeal to girls and adults are considered to be of high quality; books that appeal to boys are merely popular.

That is a gross oversimplification, of course, but not an inaccuracy. If we hope to connect boys with reading, it would serve us well to make an effort to see the world through their eyes.

Another impulse that colors our response when a boy asks for a book is the desire of many educators to encourage children to diversify their reading. This is another truly admirable goal. Its appeal is greater when working with children. It can become almost a crusade with certain boys who we see as "stuck" on certain types of literature. I cannot, however, remember any teacher, parent, or librarian distraught that a certain child is hopelessly and exclusively focused on reading the classics. Diversity is a great goal when working with children, who have the rest of their lives to read everything Orson Scott Card ever wrote. We want them to sample now and discover types of books for which they may become equally passionate if they only try them.

We must be careful, though, that our passion to "round out" a boy's reading is not a simple crusade against a type of literature we do not respect. Classics may not be a concern, and I seldom hear a girl taken to task for reading exclusively realistic fiction, but I can vividly remember a mother dropping a three-foot-high stack of books on a library return desk and begging me, "No more dinosaur books!" while her son ran for his favorite shelf. And we should recognize that if a boy reads in a narrow field, then he is reading, and a self-motivated reader is more likely to be a lifelong reader.

We must be aware, too, of the effect of pushing broader reading when the boy simply wants to read something comforting and familiar. Many boys do not read widely. They do not spend as much time as we would like reading, and that time is less productive because they may not read as well as their peers. Much of that is developmental, and when boys' brain development catches up with their female compatriots' development, they may gain both the skills and the confidence to broaden their reading. The important issue while they are still in school is to make reading a habit, a part of their lives that is valued.

One final issue of quality comes down to the age of the work. We often feel that the longer a book has been around, the better it is. There is some real wisdom here, not because writers were better two hundred years ago but because time has a way of filtering literature. There were plenty of poorly written, silly, unimportant works published one hundred years ago. Most of them have been forgotten by now. The relatively small number of works that we still remember, publish, and read from long ago are the ones large numbers of people over many generations felt were important enough to keep alive. Indeed, the most common argument I hear against the idea that we do not respect boys' literature is the number of older works that fit this category and that we revere as classics. Action and adventure stories? There is Jack London. War stories? James Fenimore Cooper. Fantasy? J. R. R. Tolkien is still considered the master. Science fiction? All right, people may at times question the absolute quality of Edgar Rice Burroughs, but what about Aldous Huxley? And humor? We consider Mark Twain to be among the greats of American letters. The classics are full of boys' literature.

Rather than this allowing us to dismiss modern books aimed at boys, it should make us reconsider these works. If London's *Call of the Wild* is an important work, then how about Ben Mikaelsen's *Touching Spirit Bear* (HarperCollins, 2001)? If Huxley's *Brave New World* stood the test of time, can we be sure that Neal Schusterman's *Unwind* (Simon and Schuster, 2007) will not? If Twain's *Tragedy of Pudd'nhead Wilson* can be both funny and worthy, can we both laugh at and respect Gordon Korman's *No More Dead Dogs* (Hyperion, 2002)?

The fact remains, many boys are more sensitive to the age of a book than either girls or adults. Maybe it is a basic distrust of the books presented to them by educators, and they simply look for any reason to reject a book. I believe that is the case, but I do not pretend to know for sure. I simply offer an observation made by myself and many other educators. Boys tend to pass on older books. When the movie series The Lord of the Rings hit the theaters, I discarded all the copies of the books I had in my library and replaced them with copies with the movie images on the covers. Usage of these books soared, and a number of boys were shocked to find they had turned the movies into books.

CONCLUSION

Concerns over the quality of literature that boys read can lead us to turn inordinately to works on personal growth and coming-of-age issues, books that have been honored with respected literary awards, works written at higher levels, and books that have proven their staying power over many generations. It is important to be aware of these qualities in literature for when the readers' advisory interview finds that such issues are the motivating force behind the request. But the appeal of these traits can be blinding. They tend to be our motivation for recommending literature but often are not a boy's motivation for reading. This is why the readers' advisory interview is so important and why we need to listen more than we talk. It is also worth doing a regular self-check: am I recommending this book because it fills the needs as expressed by the boy before me? Or am I recommending it because it is a book I want him to read?

Why is it so important that we allow the boys' interest to drive the readers' advisory encounter? Because we do not want to make reading a chore. If we push higher reading levels, try to introduce readers to types of books they are not comfortable with, or misjudge what the readers find value in, then we have turned a possibly pleasurable encounter with books into an effort with little or no immediate reward. And we have set a precedent in the boy's mind. Reading is not about one book or one experience. Readers' advisory can be a long-standing relationship but only if the boy trusts that his interests and opinions are honored. You do not do readers' advisory to get the boy a book; you do readers' advisory to make the boy a reader.

With boys, readers' advisory is often selling not just an individual title but reading itself. His relationship with reading may be in many ways about his relationship with you. Enter every readers' advisory opportunity with that in mind, and you are bound to do well. And if you do well, you may get another chance to give that boy a book next week.

CHAPTER 4

SPECIAL CIRCUMSTANCES

Readers' advisory in its purest sense is meeting the needs of a single reader. That is complicated enough, but when you add another set of needs to the equation, things can get a good deal more interesting. Whether it is someone directing the inquiry or someone there sharing in the experience, these other factors can make it difficult to focus on the needs of the boy, who you hope will ultimately read the book you hand him.

THE OUTSIDE-DIRECTED READERS' ADVISORY

Readers' advisory is probably most difficult when the reader who you must advise is not the person initiating the request for reading. The reader may then be, at best, a disinterested party, with no real investment in the transaction. At worst, the reader may be resentful and predisposed to dislike anything you offer him. The most common of these occurrences is when a teacher sends a boy in to get a book for a homework assignment.

This type of readers' advisory adds two levels of complexity. First, you must determine what is required by a teacher who is presumably not in front of you to be asked. It may take an extensive readers' advisory interview just to discover that there is an assignment from an opening inquiry that is likely to be no more helpful than "I need a book." Actually, an aggressively uninformative opener like that should lead you to begin probing for outside motivation immediately. Though it might be neither polite nor effective to ask, "Who made you need a book?" the general answer must be had. Giving a book to a boy who wants to read is very different from giving a book to a boy who is being made to read. Still, you need to get the facts straight first, so there are some extra steps to add to your readers' advisory interview.

Was there a specific title assigned? Children in general can be non-specific when dealing with adults, more so boys, who tend to be more guarded communicators. "I need a book" may very well mean "I need this specific book." Barring that showstopper of an assignment, there are many other restrictions that the teacher may have put on the choice of books that the boy may or may not be forthcoming about. Does the boy have to choose a book by a certain author or by an author with some specific trait? American author, African American author, female author, or some other characteristic?

Must the book represent a certain genre? That is a far more complicated situation than it may seem. What is the teacher's definition of that genre? There are no hard-and-fast definitions of genres, though individual teachers may have very clear definitions for their own purposes. What separates fantasy from gothic horror? Does a book written fifty years after an event qualify as historical fiction, or is it a period piece? Does a humor book qualify as realistic fiction if it is far-fetched but plausible? Add to that the modern trend to cross lines between genres, creating gothic romance and gothic humor, and the humorous science fiction of Bruce Coville. If you really want to see the problems caused by defining genres, try intimating to a serious fantasy buff that science fiction and fantasy are really part of the same genre.

The best way to avoid these confusions is to get the definition from the individual teacher. Is there a list of titles or authors to work from, either a restrictive list or one meant for examples and guidance? Is there an assignment sheet that defines what the teacher wants? If the student has no such aides, can the teacher be reached? If you must make your own distinctions, and there is any question at all, use an authoritative list and give the student the reference along with the book. Some standard sources are *Junior Genreflecting: A Guide to Good Reads and Series Fiction for Children*, by Bridget Dealy Volz, Cheryl Perkins Scheer, and Lynda Blackburn Welborn (Libraries Unlimited, 2000); *Teen Genreflecting: A Guide to Reading Interests*, by Diana Tixier Herald (Libraries Unlimited, 2003); and *Great Books for Boys*, by Kathleen Odean (Ballantine, 1998). You can use the lists that follow in this book as well; then blame me if the teacher does not agree with my definitions. Do not laugh; the boy probably plans to blame you.

Are there restrictions based on the level of reading involved? How is that level determined? If a child mentions that it must be a "fifth grade" book, then how does the teacher measure that? There are many ways to determine reading level. There are Lexile levels listed on commercial utilities such as NoveList. There are sometimes grade or age levels listed on books for guidance. Some teachers simply apply a minimum number of pages. If the teacher made a level requirement, does the student know how the teacher determines grade level?

Other factors determine the acceptability of a book for a homework assignment. One of them is simply time. When does the book need to be read by, and how long will it take the boy to read it? This might eliminate books available from another library in the system or through interlibrary loan, books checked out, and even books on the shelf if they would take too long to read. Are there assignments in addition to reading the book that must be accomplished by a deadline? This may further restrict the books you can offer because the time available for securing and reading the book may be further limited.

The second level of complexity that a homework assignment adds to readers' advisory is the need to overcome resistance occasioned by the circumstances. It is sad that, by trying to turn kids on to reading, such assignments often reinforce a dislike of reading and a distrust of those who promote reading. Researcher William Brozo has found that "choice and control are two ingredients commonly missing in instruction provided to adolescent boys who are not reading as would be expected for their grade level and who are disinterested and reluctant readers."[1] Assignments meant to expose students to certain works or to broaden their reading can often backfire with the kids who need the most encouragement, and disproportionately, that means boys.

For requests of a certain title there is obviously nothing you can do beyond making sure the assignment really is for that particular title. A boy disinterested in such an assignment may hear a suggestion and simply come in looking for that title. It is worth asking a couple of times and in a couple of different ways if indeed he must read that one book. Did the teacher mention one title but allow for other books by the same author? Or in the same genre?

If there is a range of titles available, it is important to recognize signs of resistance or disinterest. Here is where your knowledge of the available literature is important, as is your recognition that factors—in this case, gender—may affect what will appeal to the boy. A reluctant or resistant reader may require you to find books out of the mainstream of a genre and to recognize which books have those characteristics of boys' literature that are listed in this volume. Here it is especially important to include a reference, as these titles may be on the fringe of the genre and be unfamiliar or unacceptable to the teacher. By showing a boy a range of very different books, all of which qualify as "historical fiction," you can re-establish in his own mind the idea that he does in fact control what he reads.

PARENT-DIRECTED READERS' ADVISORY QUESTIONS

There are times when it is not a teacher telling a boy to get a book, but a parent. Like readers' advisory for a homework assignment, this adds extra layers of requirements that must be ferreted out during the readers' advisory interview. Many librarians may be tempted at this point to ignore the wishes of the parent and simply act as if the request comes from the child himself. The motivation here may be pure: children need to experience reading as a stress-free, self-directed activity. If they are to become lifelong readers, they need to read what, when, and how they choose.

All that is fine, but it is a central principle of librarianship that parents have the right to control their child's reading. We cannot turn that around and insist that parents only control their child's reading if we do not show good faith in preserving their rights. In addition, we serve parents as well as children, and their interests in guiding their child's reading must also be respected. The parent-directed readers' advisory question is particularly tricky because we have two very distinct customers to serve, and their interests may not match up. Indeed, they are very unlikely to, or the question would not have fallen to you.

How do you balance these two interests? That is an art, not a science. If one of these parties is standing before you and one is not, you obviously lean toward the wishes of the present party. It is a mistake, though, to ignore the interests of the other. Part of the parent's need is to find a book that engages his or her son, whatever preconceptions or restrictions the parent may place on the choice. Sending him or her home with a book the son will not read benefits nobody. Conversely, if a parent sends a child to get a book, and you give him a book the parent would not approve of, he likely will not get the chance to read the book, and you will have added stress to an already tense situation. Nobody will benefit.

This is the point where you must remember that readers' advisory is more than suggesting books. You are an advisor on reading as a process as well as a product. To be effective, you may have to educate the reader or his parents on what will help the boy to become a better reader. You will likely have to play reading therapist and listen a good deal more than you speak. The goal is to find common ground so that you can in fact find a book that serves both parties' needs. This may be particularly difficult with boys, given their tendency to find extremes in their reading that may make their parents uncomfortable. And if that is not difficult enough with one person in front of you, it becomes much more so with both. Try to remind yourself to be therapist, not judge, no matter how hard one side or the other tries to put you into that role.

READER'S ADVISORY WITH PARENTS

A parent comes to you and asks you to recommend a good book for his or her son. Simple request, right? It may seem so to the parent, even if you are fully aware of the complications. In addition to all the conflicting interests mentioned above, doing readers' advisory for a boy with only the parent present is an exercise in hearsay. Whatever information you get about the boy's interests, reading and otherwise, will be colored by the parent's perspective. That perspective may well contain a double filter, one of both age and gender.

In addition to how parents interpret the information they have, they may have a limited amount of information. Boys especially tend to keep their reading lives separate from others. They often learn that from their fathers and other male role models, as men tend to be isolated readers. The parent may have no real knowledge of what his or her son reads, how much he reads, or indeed if he reads at all. What information they have is likely to be filtered by their son. Children often tell their parents what they want to hear. Boys have a special reason to do so; they may feel their parents would not approve of what they read or respect it. They are likely to be right.

Parents may have a skewed idea of their son's reading abilities. Not having access to his reading life, many parents may defer to the boy's age or grade level. This view is skewed by the brain lag that exists between boys and girls through just about all of their school years, leaving the average boy reading below what is considered grade level. Parents may also simply have a rosy view of their child's abilities, not realizing that this blind faith may hurt the boy if the parent is constantly foisting reading material on him that is a struggle, making him feel discouraged or stupid or just that reading is more work than it is worth.

Parents of a boy who does read below grade level may be concerned that his reading does not measure up to his intelligence. Boys who succeed in many areas of school may still read at a level inconsistent with that success. Moreover, boys who apparently read well may apparently not read very much. These parents should be assured that different parts of the brain may develop at different rates and that the language areas of the brain, larger in girls than in boys anyway, may develop more slowly than other parts of a boy's brain. In addition, a boy who hides his reading may do so because he does not feel that his reading is supported or respected. Many boys who read well may still consider themselves poor readers, and some may consider their reading choices to be poor as well. Boys who apparently do not read often read quite a bit.

What does all this add up to? It means that without the boy present, it is very difficult to determine how skilled, how active, and how confident a reader he really is. Without him there, you cannot ask him to read a section for you or judge his reactions to books put before him. Instead, you must rely on the parent's view, which you know to be limited. You will also have to leverage that information with the books the boy has read recently, and that information is also likely to be filtered. Much of what a boy reads is likely to be outside of schoolwork, hidden from parents, or even nonbook.

How do you hope to serve the reading needs of a boy when you have so much filtering going on? The answer goes back to the basic approaches of the readers' advisory interview, now more important than ever. Get the parent to talk about the boy. Do not start with his reading habits, skills, or interests, but what the boy is like and what he likes to do. Parents may suddenly realize that their son does a good deal of reading associated with his interests that the parent would not have considered actual reading. If he is into sports, does he read sports magazines? If he is into gaming, does he read instruction manuals or go online to look up game cheats or participate in chat rooms or blogs about the game?

Once his interests are on the table, then you can ask about his reading experiences. Again, you are as likely here to get a series of negative comments as positive, and those negatives are important. Does the parent communicate a high level of stress around reading? Is he or she concerned about the boy or frustrated? Does he or she question the boy's choice of material or worry that the boy just is not reading at all? These are all clues. Stress may be met by humor or escapism. A boy who apparently does not read but in actuality reads in nonbook form may be best led to nonfiction. A boy who is otherwise intelligent but does not read books may respond to fantasy or science fiction. A boy who does not sit long enough to read entire books may be best introduced to action and adventure books or sports books.

If it is indeed the father of the boy before you, then you have a marvelous opportunity. Turn the discussion on him. Ask him what he reads and also what his son sees him read. So many boys are influenced by their father's reading habits that it is a wasted opportunity not to explore this. If the boy sees his father reading a certain type of book, or doing a certain type of nonbook reading, then it is worth attempting to mirror that reading for the son. Also, if you can ask the father about his reading, you can gently remind him that what he reads, and what his son sees him reading, has a great influence on the boy's reading success.

Even if the parent you see is the boy's mother, it is worth asking this question: What does the boy see his father read? Again, you face filtering issues. The mother may have a different idea of what constitutes reading than the father does, or she may have little access to his reading habits. Is the boy connected to his mother's reading life? If so, what does she read, and will she be interested in reading that day's choice with her son?

And this is just one of many advantages to having parents available for readers' advisory for their son. I do not want to make it sound like these interactions are all challenge with no upside. Parents will not only filter information about their sons but will filter information when the boy is present. With just you and a parent, the parent is more likely to discuss issues openly and freely. With some issues, such as the level of fright in a story and the resulting nightmares, they might not speak openly if they are afraid the issues will embarrass their son.

There may be issues in the boy's life that they want to deal with but do not want to put plainly before the boy. Many parents will know that boys often have difficulty addressing emotional issues directly. Whether you believe that is a product of nature or nurture, whether you agree with an indirect approach or not, many parents will seek to address the issue subtly through books. There is some argument for this. Boys' emotional viewpoints may lead them to take a one-step-removed approach to exploring their feelings. Although fantasy is often looked at as escapist literature, boys often make very real connections with issues raised in the literature specifically because they can detach those feelings from their own. A parent discussing this with a literature specialist can discuss such things more clearly without the boy present.

There is another side to this open communication. Parents may very well challenge us with their views and restrictions, free from the ears of their sons. They may express concerns and desires that do not match up with our own interests. The preferences may be as banal as a dislike of series fiction, for which we can at least try to explain the value of series in training young readers. The preferences can be more fundamental as well. The great example is the parent from a different religious background than the readers' advisor who expresses a wish not to expose his or her son to anything "unnatural," meaning anything that contains magic, talking animals, imaginary creatures, or anything else not expected in the real world.

For many readers' advisors, this is a terrible blow. We can argue about expanding the imagination, we can talk about allegory and the history of its use in literature, we can bemoan the loss of so many great books that were just on the tips of our tongues anyways, but we really should not do any of these things. The fact that we feel the parents are limiting their child, or indeed going completely overboard, is irrelevant. Insisting that the child is missing out on a world of wonderful literature is unproductive and unprincipled. Parents have the right to control their child's reading, and as a readers' advisor, we need to know that one of the criteria we must consider when recommending a book to a child is the parents' wishes.

READERS' ADVISORY WITH PARENTS
AND CHILDREN TOGETHER

We insist that we want parents involved in their children's reading, but there are limits. Sometimes the toughest situation is facing a parent and child together, especially when they disagree about what should come of the readers' advisory encounter. In short, they want you to play referee. You cannot allow that to happen. You are an advisor and have no authority beyond what is given to you by the people you serve. It is essential to always assert both the value of control over one's own reading and the vital role of the parent in encouraging and guiding a child's reading, even if these two ideals are in direct conflict. If you feel pressured to make a ruling, just keep repeating those two ideals, and hope for the best.

That said, it is the boy who will be reading the book you suggest, so you should try to carry on the readers' advisory interview with him as much as possible. Ultimately, the most useful approach is to get the boy talking. That goal is made more difficult when the parents try to answer questions on behalf of the son or try too hard to impose their conditions. Remember, you are serving two different audiences here. There is the boy, who wants to find something that meets his needs, and the parents, who have an honest interest in guiding their child's reading. Although you may be tempted to try to split the two at this point, you would be doing so for your comfort, not for the best interest of your customers. The best way to serve both is to act as a role model, allowing the parent to see how you elicit the interests of the boy and allowing the boy to see you can honor his interests, meet the expectations of the parent, and still come up with something interesting to read.

Even if you manage to give the boy the floor, you need to always keep in mind that the information you are getting may be colored by the presence of a parent. The boy could simply be telling you what he thinks Mom or Dad wants to hear, or conversely, he may say things just to drive his parents crazy. Body language may be a help. If a boy is constantly checking back to the parent, then he is likely speaking with an eye to how his words are being interpreted. Look for agitation on either party's part.

Perhaps worse than the colored information you may receive is the harm that comes from things not said. Parents and boys alike may reserve their concerns, not wanting to express them in front of the other. If nobody is talking, then you cannot really do an effective readers' advisory interview. This is the time to set the boy looking through a shelf of books while you take the parent aside; then reverse the positions so that both can talk to you about what is on their minds.

One last thing to consider, a father may be carrying emotional baggage from his time as a boy, baggage that may color his view of reading, school assignments, libraries, and you. Libraries were once less friendly to boys than they are now, and many men carry an assumption that librarians will dictate good reading rather than engage readers. They may then hang back, not expressing themselves. If they wait and express their displeasure with a reading choice later, after the boy has left the library, then the readers' advisory encounter will have been a failure. It is best to engage a reluctant parent as well as a reluctant reader.

The downside of getting both child and parent to speak up is that they are likely to express mutually exclusive wants and needs. The possible points of contention begin with reading level and length of the book, issues of quality and popularity, even the look of the cover. You should remember that it is not always possible to make everyone happy. You should take the opportunity to offer a broad range of titles and the value-added service of a good booktalk or two. You do not have to see the boy and the parent come to a consensus, and you never have to cast the deciding vote. Stress to both that reading is an ongoing adventure. They can take a number of books home, start all of them, and finish the one or ones that appeal the most. Most important, the readers' advisory service does not end in one encounter. Encourage the two to extend the transaction into a regular conversation; invite them back for round two.

CONCLUSION

Not all readers' advisory encounters involve serving a self-motivated reader looking for a book for his own enjoyment. There may be others who have an interest in the book the boy selects, and each of these exterior interests makes the process that much more challenging but also that much more effective. Although school assignments may attempt to make boys well read, good readers' advisory can make those assignments powerful tools to make boys good readers. As challenging as readers' advisory with parents may be, by role modeling for parents the process of matching boys to books that speak to them, we leverage our efforts and expand our effectiveness. A boy's motivation when looking for a book may have nothing to do with a desire to read, but the end result may still be a love of reading. A final plea: whenever you perform readers' advisory, allow your love for reading to be plain and visible. Maybe it will inspire parents and teachers to do the same.

NOTE

1. Brozo quoted in Donna Lester Taylor, "'Not Just Boring Stories': Reconsidering the Gender Gap for Boys," *Journal of Adolescent and Adult Literacy* (December/January, 2005): 294.

CHAPTER 5

BOOKTALKING FOR BOYS

The ultimate readers' advisory is, of course, the booktalk. Whether it is done one-on-one in the stacks of the library or standing before an entire room full of kids, there are times when we just need to sell a book. Do not ever forget that booktalking is not book reviewing. You are under no obligation to give a full and fair account of the book. You are trying to convince kids to read the book.

There are two sides to this. On one hand, you are selling the book. On the other hand, you may be selling reading itself. When addressing a class full of kids, remember that your audience is split, either physically or psychologically, into the front of the class and the back of the class. The front of the class are those students who are already avid readers, have probably read every book in their homes, in the classroom library, and maybe in the school and public libraries. Ignore them. They will respond to anything you present anyway. They just need another book.

Instead, address yourself to the back of the class, those kids who do not read for pleasure, who have no relationship with books, and who frankly have no intention of listening to you. These may be the hardest kids to reach, but they are also the ones who most need you to reach them. If you say to these kids, "The next time you pick up a good book, this would be a good book to pick up," their likely response would be, "That's fine. I have no intention of picking up a book anytime soon, but I'll keep that in mind." You need to do so much more. You need to give these kids a reason to read before you give them a book to read.

Booktalking, though, is readers' advisory on the cheap. You are not trying to meet the needs of an individual reader, and you cannot perform a readers' advisory interview. Booktalking must be engaging, entertaining, and fun—all the things that the most reluctant readers think reading is not. For boys especially, booktalking is an opportunity to change their experience with reading. To that end, I offer these rules when booktalking to boys.

KEEP IT SHORT

Always keep it short. If you spend twenty minutes going on and on about how wonderful a book is, there will be a boy in the back of the class thinking, "Oh, man, how long will it take me to read it?" I had the great pleasure of booktalking on a regular basis with a colleague who was the opposite of me. She was short, quiet, and loved all the most girlie of the girlie books. She would booktalk her books her way, and I would booktalk my books my way. She would booktalk for ten minutes; I would booktalk for ten minutes. She would booktalk one book; I would booktalk seven books.

I have never believed that it takes a long time to describe a book. You may at times read a substantial passage from a book if the writing itself is the draw and you want the kids to experience that language, but more often you should find the "hook" and present it to kids with as little distraction as possible. Once you have a listener hooked, all you can accomplish by prolonging the booktalk is to turn him off to the book. Corollary to that, if I am booktalking and a kid raises his hand, I stop talking and hand him the book. This can create some funny situations in a classroom booktalking situation. Kids realize that the most engaging books are going quickly, and they start raising their hands earlier and earlier. The frenzy resembles the atmosphere in an exciting auction. Eventually, you will open your mouth to start a booktalk and a hand will fly up before you can say a word. Enjoy it; you have now successfully sold the idea of reading itself.

You can increase the pace of your booktalking by having related books in reserve for each book that you booktalk. Have other books in the series, other books by the author, or other books in the same genre. When the fastest kid gets the book you booktalk, you can hold up a handful more and say, "And who wants . . . ?" In this way I have handed out thirty, forty, and even more titles in a single booktalking session.

GET THEM INVOLVED

Which brings us to the next rule for when booktalking to boys: always have copies the kids can take with them of the books you present. Whether you booktalk books from the classroom library or have books from the school or public library that the kids can check out right there, or you just have books to give away, you need to put books in the kids' hands while they are excited about the books. It does no good to sell a kid on a book and then tell him he needs to go find a copy. That will work for an excited, engaged reader, but that is not your intended audience.

Engage your audience in your booktalks. Many boys remember story hour and kindergarten as the last time they enjoyed reading. That is at least partly because reading then was an interactive, engaging activity. Reading was done in groups, out loud, and with fun activities connected to the story. Give them back that experience, and they may dig up all those fond memories and make your job a good deal easier.

An interactive booktalk helped me to escape a tight spot. Some years ago, a middle school in a small New Hampshire town asked me to come in and booktalk to all their seventh- and eighth-grade classes, two classes per session, five sessions in one day. And they gave me a theme to work with: leadership. I hope it is obvious that this is the kind of theme adults, especially educators, believe will appeal to adolescents. Clearly, that is misguided. The prospect of spending five hours booktalking on the theme of leadership to twelve- and thirteen-year-olds had me losing sleep for days before the event. In the wee hours of the morning on the day of the event, an idea came to me to bail myself out of this mess.

I remembered that I had a new book on my desk at work and had been working out a plan for a booktalk. The book was *The Worst-Case Scenario Survival Handbook,* by Joshua Piven and David Borgenicht (Chronicle, 1999). Leadership brought to mind the Boy Scout motto, "Be prepared." I could sell that.

I stood before the first group of the day with the book behind my back and asked for a volunteer. No one raised a hand, of course. I cajoled one student into coming forward, and when he stood in front of the class I said to him, "You are swimming in the ocean when you feel a shark bite your leg. He's still holding on; what do you do?"

An explosion of laughter, and the victim said, "I'd scream."

"That will make you feel better," I said, "But it won't make the shark let go. You're dead. Sit down."

More peals of laughter and a dozen or more hands shot up in the air. "Punch him in the nose!" one student yelled. I told the group that this was what was done in the movies but that scientists have found that sharks have little feeling in their noses, so that kid was dead, too. Eventually, someone suggested punching the shark in the eye, and that was the right answer. How did I know? I produced the book and explained that all the questions and all the answers, right or wrong, were in this book. I then asked for another volunteer. This time, there was no shortage.

We faced down bears and mountain lions and drove a car into a lake, among other adventures. After twenty minutes I went to put down the book to reach for another and a most amazing thing happened. The class stood up as one in protest. "I didn't get a turn," many of the students cried, the same ones who would not raise their hands when I started. I was able to deliver the best line in booktalking: "Read the book." I told them to get a copy of the book, gather five friends, and play the game. Flip to a random page, read the scenario, and see who could come up with the correct answer.

The same scene played out five times that day. As each class began, students were sitting on their hands; by the end, they were crying for more. A week later I received an e-mail from the school librarian saying she had to order twelve copies of the book just to keep the reserve list down to a reasonable length.

Another favorite interactive booktalk uses Joy Masoff's *Oh Yuck! The Encyclopedia of Everything Nasty* (Workman, 2000). Simply ask a kid to pick a number between 1 and 199. Whatever number he chooses, open the book to that page and read the first headline and its paragraph. You are nearly assured of reading something that is fascinating, funny, gross, and possibly all of the above. You can do this in a group or one-on-one. With a single kid, take turns reading out loud. Use it as a reward. Every teacher and librarian could have a copy in his or her desk, and when some kid does something great, or just needs a pick-me-up, pull out the book and ask him to pick a number.

One positive outcome of this approach is that many kids will go looking for their own copy of the book and read through the whole thing looking for the best page numbers to throw at you. Is there a better outcome for a booktalk than this, that kids are motivated to read the book independently? A word of caution, though; read the entire book yourself first. Make sure there is nothing in it you would not read aloud. Whether by reading the book themselves, or pure childish instinct, kids will choose the pages with the most disgusting entries. If you tell a kid to pick a page, and you look up the page and then tell him to pick another, he will never trust you again. The last time I made the offer in a middle school, the child picked "Rocky Mountain Oysters." If you cannot bring yourself to talk about eating bull testicles, you are not ready for this particular booktalk.

FOCUS ON BOY APPEAL

Highlight the aspects of the book that are most likely to appeal to boys. It is not enough to booktalk a book that boys will like; you must booktalk it in a way they will respond to as well. At a conference for librarians, I watched the owners of a local independent bookstore presenting boy-friendly titles to the attendees. To my delight, one of the booksell-ers held up *Rescue Josh McGuire* (Hyperion, 1991), a fantastic action and adventure story by Ben Mikaelsen about a boy who runs away to live in the woods with his pet bear cub to save the cub from an evil man who wants to kill it. But instead of talking about the plot of the story, the book-seller spent twenty minutes discussing the relationship between the boy in the story and his father.

If you are selling an action and adventure story, highlight the action and adventure. If you are selling a funny book, make your audience laugh. If it is a sports book, talk about the sports. If it is a book about inner-city race relations and the power of friendship to overcome hatred, talk about the sports! (See my booktalk on Jerry Spinelli's *Maniac Magee* in chapter 7, "Booktalks for Middle School Boys.") You are under no obligation to give a fair, complete, and balanced assessment of the book. Your goal is to get the kids to read it. Let them discover the joy. If you need to trick them to do it, I hope you are willing to do so.

One of the most influential readers' advisory encounters I had as an adolescent came when a high school librarian put a brown paper envelope on the circulation desk and slid it across to me. "Don't," she cautioned, "tell anyone I gave you that book." I was intrigued, slipped the package under my arm, took it back to my room, and spent the next two days read-ing that book cover to cover, looking for the good parts. There were none. The book was *The Hobbit*, by J. R. R. Tolkien (Graphia, 2002). That librarian recognized that I would be reluctant to read a book that she felt would affect me deeply, so she simply lied to me to get me to read it. It worked. I spent the next few weeks reading the entire Lord of the Rings series, and I have been an avid Tolkien fan ever since.

When we booktalk, librarians quite often zero in on the characters in the book and their interpersonal relations. Most children's librarians are women, and this is what we, as a group, feel is most important and interesting about books. We also tend to make booktalks very long and

---

MICHAEL SULLIVAN'S RULES FOR BOOK TALKING TO BOYS

- Booktalking is not book reviewing; sell the book.
- Keep it short.
- Booktalk books that the kids can have right then.
- Involve the audience in your booktalks.
- Highlight the things that appeal to boys.
- Favor plot over characterization.

intricate, as if we can reveal all that is great about an entire book with a single booktalk. We need to explore different styles of booktalks, so even if one booktalk will not appeal to all, our booktalking as a whole will reach a broad audience. In addition, if we want to reach boys, it is a good idea to keep the booktalks short. Girls are more likely to be drawn in by an emotional setup; boys are looking for the impact. What follows in the next three chapters are approaches to booktalking that will appeal specifically to boys, along with illustrative examples of my favorite booktalks.

CONCLUSION

Boys often think of reading as solitary, sedentary, and feminized. Although that is certainly not true for all boys, it is true for enough of them and certainly so for the boys who are the most reluctant or resistant as readers. Booktalking gives us a chance to challenge those perceptions, but only if we recognize them and take them head-on. In all my years of booktalking, I have never walked out of a classroom with a book; there has always been some kid to take any book. That is an incredibly powerful tool for reaching readers. We need to booktalk well, and we need to booktalk often. Every program in your library should start with one or two booktalks, and you should have one or two more ready for the end of the program as well. During every media appearance, find a way to sneak in a booktalk. Every encounter you have with a boy is a chance to turn him on to reading; use it. If you cannot get excited about giving books to boys, then boys may never see what is appealing in books.

CHAPTER 6

BOOKTALKS FOR ELEMENTARY SCHOOL BOYS

Kevin Bolger. *Sir Fartsalot Hunts the Booger.* **Penguin, 2008.**

Why do kids think farts are hilariously funny? Because farts are hilariously funny! (I stole that one from Dennis Miller.) This is slapstick humor with far too many bodily function jokes for comfort (did you notice that the author's name is one letter away from *booger*?). And you can't judge a book by its cover, but everybody does, and the hologram cover is just too cool.

Eoin Colfer. *Legend of Spud Murphy.* **Miramax, 2004.**

"Don't make us join the library," Marty begged. "It's too dangerous."
"Dangerous? How could a library be dangerous?" Dad asked.
"It's not the library," Marty whispered. "It's the librarian."
"Mrs. Murphy?" said Mom. "She's a lovely old lady."
"She's not a lovely old lady," I said. "She's a total nut."
"Will! That's a terrible thing to say."
"But she is, Mom. She hates kids and she used to be a spy in the army. Tracking kids from enemy countries."
"She has a spud gun under her desk," added Marty. "A gas-powered one that takes an entire potato in the barrel. She shoots kids with it if they make a noise in the library. That's why we call her Spud Murphy." (pp. 8–12)

Bruce Coville. *Aliens Ate My Homework.* **Alien Adventures series. Minstrel, 1993.**

Rod Allbright has three problems: (1) the schoolyard bully keeps smashing bugs in his hair; (2) the most-wanted criminal in the entire galaxy is hiding somewhere in his neighborhood; and (3) five aliens hiding in his room just ate a hole in his science fair project . . . So, which one do you think he should take care of first?

Erik Craddock. *Stone Rabbit: B.C. Mambo.* **Stone Rabbit series. Random House, 2009.**

A prehistoric farce of a graphic novel about a rabbit, a bottle of barbeque sauce, an evil caveman-genius who wants to rule the world, and an army of wind-up killer robots. No, the boys won't enjoy this!

Kathleen Duey. Time Soldiers series. Big Guy Books.

You know how science fiction goes: someone takes off, to another time or another place, and comes back with wild tales of amazing people or unbelievable creatures. The traveler may even draw you a picture to show you what it's like. But these kids come back with photographs and even video! Dinosaurs, pirates, knights in armor. Seeing is believing.

David Elliott. *The Transmogrification of Roscoe Wizzle.* **Candlewick, 2001.**

Transmogrify: "To change or transform, especially into something funny or comical" (p. 28). You know, like when children eat too many hamburgers and turn into bugs.

Alternate Booktalk

"I used to be a normal kid. I mean, don't get me wrong, I still am normal. But once you get changed into a bug, you do see things a little bit differently . . ." (p. 8). So says Roscoe Wizzle in *The Transmogrification of Roscoe Wizzle,* by David Elliott.

D. L. Garfinkle. *Fowl Language.* **Supernatural Rubber Chicken series. Mirrorstone, 2008.**

He stinks, he is lying on a pile of dirty boxer shorts, and every word out of his mouth is a nasty insult. This is *not* Cinderella's fairy godmother. But Ed the supernatural rubber chicken can grant wishes. Is he Nate and Lisa's dream come true? Or is he their worst nightmare? That depends on whether they can get the right wish to the right person, or if their wishes all go haywire. Hey, what's the chance that a supernatural rubber chicken might mess up a wish? About as good as the chance that D. L. Garfinkle's series will make you fall out of your seat laughing.

Dan Gutman. *The Get Rich Quick Club.* **HarperCollins, 2004.**

Q: If you sold lemonade at 25 cents a glass, how many glasses would you have to sell to make a million dollars?

A: 4 million glasses of lemonade!

Q: If you washed cars for two dollars a car, how many cars would you have to wash to make a million dollars?

A: Five hundred thousand cars!

Q: If a UFO landed in front of you, how many pictures of it would you have to sell to make a million dollars?

A: One!

Dan Gutman. *Satch & Me.* **Baseball Card Mysteries series. HarperCollins, 2006.**

> "This is the great Josh Gibson. The Bronzed Bambino. Prob'bly the greatest hitter in baseball history. Hey Josh, is it true you hit 84 homers in 1936? Is it true you batted .600 one year?"
>
> "It's true," Gibson sighed. "All of it."
>
> "Numbers don't mean nothin'," one of the other players said. "I remember this one time we were playin' in Pittsburgh and Josh hit one outta sight. Looked like it was never gonna come down. The next day we were playin' in Philly and this ball comes flying out of the sky. Somebody caught it and the ump says to Josh, 'Yer out! Yesterday in Pittsburgh!'" (pp. 57–58)

Bruce Hale. *The Big Nap: A Chet Gecko Mystery.* **From the Tattered Casebook of Chet Gecko, Private Eye series. Harcourt, 2001.**

Something was very wrong at Emerson Hicky Elementary school. What could make otherwise normal wisecracking goof-offs clean blackboards, study during recess, and actually pay attention during science class? I mean, this was weird. Everywhere, students were walking stiff-legged and slow, with a dazed look in their eyes, saying things like "School good" and "Must study" and "Must help teacher. Teacher good." Who could be behind it? Could it be the furry kid in the magician's hat practicing hypnosis? The smooth-talking new weasel in town? Or could it be that really big new librarian with the dark glasses, a funny way of talking, and all the books on zombies? Whoever it is, they better watch out, because for seventy-five cents and all the mosquito milk shakes he can drink, Chet Gecko, private eye, is on the case.

Peter Lerangis. *Poof! Rabbits Everywhere!* **Abracadabra! series. Scholastic, 2001.**

When a rabbit pops up in school out of nowhere, it's pretty funny. When three show up, it's distracting. When five show up, it's annoying. When seven show up, the principal of Rebus Elementary School threatens to kick the Abracadabra Club out of school unless they can prove they really aren't pulling these rabbits out of their hats. Maybe the person to blame is the suspicious looking man from the magic shop who has been putting on disguises and hanging around school, but they better find some proof soon, or it is the magic club that will disappear, in *Poof! Rabbits Everywhere!*

David Lubar. *Punished!* Darby Creek, 2006.

> Mr. Vernack pointed to the vocabulary list on the board. "Logan, the first word is isolate. Can you use it in a sentence?"
>
> "Sure," I said. "I'm sorry isolate getting here."
>
> Everyone started laughing. Everyone except Mr. Vernack. He frowned and gave me the next word. Justice.
>
> "Justice I was leaving home, my dog got loose."
>
> Mr. Vernack's frown grew so big, his eyes became slits. He said one word: "Decide."
>
> "My dog chased a cat around decide of my house."
>
> "Logan, is this some kind of joke?" Mr. Vernack asked.
>
> "No, Mister Vernack. I was jest doing wit you asked." I clamped my mouth shut. Nothing seemed to be coming out right.
>
> He stared at me for a long time. Then he sighed and said, "Very well, I'll give you one more chance. The next word is industry."
>
> That was easy. There was no way I could mess it up. "The cat got stuck up industry and wouldn't come down." (pp. 26–27)

Puns are great, but what if you couldn't stop making them? To your friends, your parents, your teachers, even your principal. Logan has to complete three Herculean tasks of language lunacy or face a life where no one will ever take him seriously in *Punished!* by David Lubar.

Mike Lupica. *Two-Minute Drill*. Mike Lupica's Comeback Kids series. Philomel, 2007.

Two-Minute Drill is the story of the proverbial last kid picked for the pickup game, but this kid has one special skill that could make all the difference in the big game if he can only hold on long enough to get to those all-important last two minutes.

A. A. Milne. *The House at Pooh Corner.* Puffin, 1992.

> "Rabbit is clever," said Pooh thoughtfully.
>
> "Yes," said Piglet, "Rabbit is clever."
>
> "And he has Brain."
>
> "Yes," said Piglet, "Rabbit has Brain."
>
> "I suppose," said Pooh, "that that's why he never understands anything."
> (p. 131)

Mary Elise Monsell. Pictures by Lynn Munsinger. *Underwear!* Whitman, 1988.

[Hide the book behind your back.] I have the funniest book ever written in my hand. This book is so hilariously funny that children older than you have been known to turn purple and pass out just looking at the pictures.

Scientists at NASA have failed to adequately explain how this book got to be just this funny. No living human being has ever been able to read this book, out loud, without laughing so hard their spleen burst. Sadly, tragically, thousands have tried and paid the price. Are you ready for the challenge? Can you do it without laughing? Do you dare read . . . *Underwear!?* [Reveal the book.]

Laurie Myers. *Surviving Brick Johnson.* **Clarion, 2000.**

Alex carries baseball cards to help him through his day. They inspire him. If he wants to be fast, he carries the card of a fast player, like Barry Bonds. If he wants to be alert, he carries the catcher Mike Piazza. Now Brick Johnson—the biggest kid in school—is out to maim him, and Alex needs a very special card, one that will inspire him to greatness . . . Who would you choose?

Alternate Booktalk

Alex thinks that Brick Johnson, the biggest kid in school, is going to maim him. The only problem is, he doesn't know what *maim* means, so he looks it up in the dictionary.

> "maim. 1. to cause serious physical injury"
> Yep. That made sense. Brick did want to cause him serious physical injury. The second and third definitions were worse.
> "maim. 2. to disable or make defective."
> "maim. 3. to deprive a person of a limb or member of the body"
> "Mom, exactly how important are the second and third definitions of a word?"
> "It depends on the word." (pp. 6–7)

That was the answer Alex hated most. It depends . . . Brick would know all the possible definitions for *maim*. Maybe Brick was planning all three!

Ken Roberts. *The Thumb in the Box.* **Douglas and McIntyre, 2001.**

The little village of New Auckland, Canada, has one girl who knows everything . . . one boy who can't stop smiling . . . one fire truck stuck in the mud . . . zero roads . . . one African lion . . . a severe shortage of playground equipment . . . one world-famous painter . . . and a man who can take off his thumb and put it in a box. Find out what it all means in *The Thumb in the Box,* by Ken Roberts.

Ken Roberts. *Thumb on a Diamond.* **Groundwood, 2006.**

Explain to me how to get on and off an elevator, if I've never seen one.

I'm sitting in a restaurant for the first time ever, and someone is holding a pen and a pad of paper and staring at me. What do I do?

OK, now tell me how to play baseball if I've never played, or even seen, a game.

The New Auckland Beavers are about to play in the Provincial Middle School Baseball Championship. Unfortunately, they have never played baseball.

Jon Scieszka. *Sam Samurai.* **The Time Warp Trio series. Viking, 2001.**

> The Samurai scowled down at us. "No one disturbs our master's peace with their entertainments unless they ask me, leader of the Red Devil bodyguards, Owattabutt." The samurai posed proudly.
>
> Fred's eyes bugged out. I couldn't stop him.
>
> "Oh what a butt?" asked Fred.
>
> "Owattabutt of Minowa," said the samurai.
>
> "Oh—what a butt," repeated Sam.
>
> We tried our best not to laugh. We really did. But you know us.
>
> It took us about three seconds to crack up, freak out Owattabutt, have our hands tied behind our backs, and get surrounded by a gang of red samurai warriors with spears.
>
> Then things really went bad. (p. 55)

How could they get worse? Read *Sam Samurai,* by Jon Scieszka, and find out.

Jon Scieszka. *Summer Reading Is Killing Me.* **The Time Warp Trio series. Viking, 1998.**

As if the title wasn't enough, Winnie-the-Pooh gets carried off by Dracula, and the librarian is really the devil.

Michael Sullivan. *Escapade Johnson and Mayhem at Mount Moosilauke.* **Escapade Johnson series. PublishingWorks, 2006.**

> Melinda was sitting across from me, going through a tree identification guide and drawing leaves in her notebook. I strained my neck as she flipped through a few pages and saw drawings of flowers, animal tracks, and . . .
>
> "Poop!" I said, a little louder than I wanted to. All conversation stopped, and I mean immediately.
>
> Melinda glared up at me. "It's called scat."
>
> "In my world, it's called poop."
>
> "When animals do it in the woods, it's called scat, and it's one way of knowing what animal species are in the environment."
>
> "Wow," said Davy, "that has to be the only time you could tell someone their drawings look like crap and it would be a compliment." (pp. 34–35)

Escapade Johnson's name may mean adventure, but he is the most boring kid in Sanbornton Elementary School in Sanbornton, New Hampshire, which means he is the most boring kid in the most boring town in the most boring state in the country.

So how does he end up setting the town's only fire truck on fire, feeding the whole town's ballots to a moose at the last election, hunting witches in the woods, and staring down a bear on the side of a mountain?

Begin the adventure with *Escapade Johnson and Mayhem at Mount Moosilauke.*

Hudson Talbott. *Safari Journal: The Adventures in Africa of Carey Monroe.* **Silver Whistle, 2003.**

Carey Monroe, on safari in Africa:

> The road I followed leads to a little village on the other side of the creek. There's a kid over there watching me. He looks about my age. I wonder if he's ever seen a Frisbee. I took mine out of my pack and tossed it over the creek. He picked it up and threw it right back. The next time I threw it he caught it and sent it right back to me. We were tossing it back and forth until—SPLASH—it had to happen—it landed right in the middle of the creek. I started to wade in for it, but the kid went nuts!
>
> "No! No! Mamba! Mamba!" he was yelling at me. And I'm thinking, "Who's Mamba?"
>
> My newest Swahili word: Mamba = Crocodile!
>
> Out of nowhere two giant jaws chomped down on my Frisbee! (n.p.).

Vivian Vande Velde. *Wizard at Work.* **Magic Carpet Books, 2003.**

So, what did you do on your summer vacation? All this particular wizard wanted to do was work in his garden and fish. He didn't want to deal with princesses in peril, curses, ghosts, or sea monsters, and he *certainly* didn't want a princess tagging along while he dealt with the curse of the ghost of a sea monster, but for a wizard, it's all in a day's work.

Desiree Webber. *The Buffalo Train Ride.* **Eakin, 1999.**

Would you share a cramped train car with a buffalo? Or five? You might if it meant a chance to save these magnificent animals and return them to a life of roaming the American plains. This is the true story of the men who preserved one of the great symbols of America.

CHAPTER 7

BOOKTALKS FOR MIDDLE SCHOOL BOYS

Avi. *Crispin: Cross of Lead.* **Hyperion, 2002.**

Can you imagine having no family, no home, not even a name? What do you have left? Well, for this orphan boy in medieval England, all he has is a simple cross about his neck and a terrible secret that he doesn't even know that makes him a hunted animal. This is a story of going out on the road, finding strange friends, and trying to find yourself in a harsh world.

Dave Barry and Ridley Pearson. *Peter and the Starcatchers.* **Disney, 2004.**

Bloodthirsty pirates, hidden treasures, lost civilizations, and giant flying alligators . . . What's not to love?

Andrew Clements. *A Week in the Woods.* **Simon and Schuster, 2002.**

One of these guys is the gung-ho cheerleader type, you know, rah rah rah, let's show some spirit and all that. One is sullen and moody and way too bored with school. One of these guys is a go-get-'em science teacher. The other is a slacker student with a bad attitude. One is an outdoorsy environmentalist type. The other is more comfortable in a New York penthouse than he is in a tent in New Hampshire. One lives on a schoolteacher's salary. The other gets driven to school in a limousine. Oh yeah, these two are going to get along great when they spend a week in the woods.

Christopher Paul Curtis. *The Watsons Go to Birmingham—1963.* **Delacorte, 1995.**

Take to the open road with the Weird Watsons in an old Plymouth called the Brown Bomber, complete with an onboard record player blaring "Yakety Yak" all the way. You'll go from the neighborhood antics of downtown

Flint, Michigan, to the explosive center of the Deep South in the midst of the civil rights movement. Travel with Daniel, Wilona, Kenny, Joey, and Daddy Cool through the everyday adventures of growing up—and the once-in-a-lifetime experience of being smack-dab in the middle of history. From Christopher Paul Curtis, it's *The Watsons Go to Birmingham—1963*.

Ann Downer. *Hatching Magic*. Aladdin, 2003.

Gideon the magician has lost his dragon. Actually, the dragon lost herself, off to go have her baby in peace. Gideon must figure out where, and when, to look for her before his rival gets his hands on her and turns her against him. The *where* turns out to be Cambridge, Massachusetts. The *when* happens to be present day. The rival happens to be right on Gideon's heels. Can two magicians (and one cranky demon in high-heeled shoes) from thirteenth-century England find a dragon in twenty-first-century America? Find out in *Hatching Magic,* by Ann Downer.

Emily Drake. *The Magickers*. The Magickers series. DAW, 2001.

Camp Ravenwyng is just like any other summer camp. It has cabins, counselors, a lake, arts and crafts, and campfires. Of course, one of the cabins is haunted . . . one of the counselors hovers a foot above the ground . . . the lake has a sea monster . . . arts and crafts includes learning how to use magic crystals . . . and the campfires are held under the gathering clouds of a magical storm that could signal the end of the world as we know it.

Jeanne DuPrau. *The City of Ember*. Books of Ember series. Random House, 2003.

Your city is dying. Food is short, new clothes nonexistent. Even lightbulbs, your one weapon against the constant darkness, are hard to come by. Would you plunge into the unknown for the slimmest chance to escape? Even if you can escape, could you leave behind everyone and everything you have ever known? Would you go into the darkness just to find the light?

Nancy Farmer. *Sea of Trolls*. Atheneum, 2004.

These guys are nuts. In fact, they are Bizerkers. When they go into battle, they lose all control, all restraint. They kill and burn and rampage, and no one can stop them; they can't even stop themselves. They want to die in battle and go to the glorious halls of Valhalla, where they can feast and fight forever and ever. How do you reason with people like that? You don't. How do you survive people like that? You scare them into believing you have magic, and you let them imagine just what you can do to them if they make you mad. But, of course, who better to send on a dangerous quest than a powerful magician? Now you have to survive carnivorous plants, huge trolls, and man-eating beasts instead.

John Feinstein. *Cover-Up: Mystery at the Super Bowl.*
Knopf, 2007.

Steve Thomas and Susan Carol Anderson are fourteen-year-old sports fans with the dream job. They get to cover all the biggest sporting events as sports reporters. Now they are on TV and covering the biggest sports event of all: the Super Bowl. But these two never get to enjoy the game, what with major scandals and people trying to kill them and all. Here is a story of big-time, big-money, big-pressure sports and the two teenagers who have to save the game for everyone.

John Flanagan. *The Battle for Skandia.* **Ranger's Apprentice series, book 4. Philomel, 2008.**

They have battled beasts of unspeakable horror, and dark magic bent on covering the world with its thrall, but Halt and Will, Ranger and apprentice, must face a terror all too human. The Temujai are a fearless and selfless horde that have never been defeated in battle, because they fight by the thousands as if they were a single sword. The civilized world is threatened with extinction unless the Temujai are stopped at a line in the sand, and all Will and Halt have to stop them is a thin strip of land and an unruly bunch of adventurers and thieves. Teaching time is over; the Ranger's Apprentice is going to war.

John Flanagan. *The Burning Bridge.* **Ranger's Apprentice series, book 2. Philomel, 2006.**

Sacrifice: it means to step between. To put yourself over the abyss so that others may pass safely. *Sacrifice* is like a bridge over a huge chasm. In *The Burning Bridge,* book 2 of John Flanagan's Ranger's Apprentice series, both Will, the apprentice ranger, and Horace, the apprentice soldier, step into the gap. As young as they are, they can stand where all the adults cannot. The bridge in the story is the link that will allow the evil Lord Morgorath to march his armies into the heart of the peaceful world, and it needs to come down. One apprentice will take on the bridge; one will take on Morgorath himself. But danger is in the nature of sacrifice; the two young heroes will step into the breach, and one will not come back.

Tim Green. *Football Genius.* **HarperCollins, 2007.**

A fantastical football book from a real professional football player. Is football a game of physical strength or football smarts? More rests on the answer to that question than you may think: people's jobs, their careers, the hopes of one middle school football genius, and the season of the Atlanta Falcons. But how do you convince a professional football team that they need the help of a scrawny kid with a neat parlor trick?

Dan Gutman. *Getting Air.* **Simon and Schuster, 2007.**

What do you call
>a couple of skateboarding guys who are forced to wear dresses . . .
>a stewardess who is forced to eat bugs . . .
>and a grandmother who just lost all her friends in a plane crash?
>In Dan Gutman's *Getting Air,* you'd call them the lucky ones.

Julie Hahnke. *The Grey Ghost.* **The Wolf's Apprentice series. PublishingWorks, 2009.**

Five hundred years ago, Black Duncan Campbell is out to exterminate Clan Macnab, and he very nearly does it. Seven-year-old Angus is the sole survivor, but he is not alone. He has the history of his clan, and some magical creatures to guide and aid him, but what can a boy, a pine marten, a hawk, and a luna moth do against the greatest tyrant Scotland has ever known? They can fight to the last, and that is what they pledge to do in this, the first book in a new series based on Scottish history and mythology.

Sid Hite. *Stick & Whittle.* **Scholastic, 2000.**

What are the chances that two guys named Melvin would run into each other in the vast open plains of Indian country? What are the chances that a soldier who has been gone for eight years could find his long-lost sweetheart when all he knows is that she is somewhere out West? And what are the chances that a dead man, two teenagers, and one old Indian could rescue the captives from a band of well-armed desperadoes in a heavily fortified canyon? Well, when Stick and Whittle are involved, anything is possible.

Will Hobbs. *Go Big or Go Home.* **HarperCollins, 2008.**

With a meteor named Fred, a giant trout named Stan, a war dog named Attila, super germs from Mars, and a toilet-chucking catapult, Will Hobbs takes his own advice in *Go Big or Go Home.*

Will Hobbs. *Wild Man Island.* **HarperTrophy, 2002.**

Here is an adventure story that has it all:
>Sea kayaking in Alaska . . .
>Getting lost in a deserted wilderness . . .
>Huge brown bears . . .
>And a wild man running around in animal skins and waving a stone
spear.
>Read it now so you will be ready when they make the movie.

Alternate Booktalk

Wilderness. Under the circumstances, I couldn't imagine a more ominous word, unless it was bears. What else did I know about Admiralty Island? "All three of the ABC Islands have brown bears," Julia had said early in the trip. I knew for an awful fact that the bear I'd just seen was a monster grizzly. Brown bears, the naturalist had gone on to explain, were the same animal as grizzlies—Ursus arctos. Brownies, as Julia called them, got a lot bigger in southeast Alaska than the grizzlies in the interior because of all the extra protein that salmon added to their diet. Some topped a thousand pounds.

Tell me about it.

Julia said there was another name for Admiralty, the Indian name. The Indians called it the Fortress of the Bears.

I felt sick, remembering what she'd said next. "Admiralty Island has the densest population of brown bears in the world. One per square mile." (pp. 36–37)

And Andy Galloway has just washed up on the shore of Admiralty Island, the Fortress of the Bears.

Thomas R. Holtz and Luis V. Rey. *Dinosaurs: The Most Complete, Up-to-Date Encyclopedia for Dinosaur Lovers of All Ages.* Random House, 2007.

I know, we have lots of dinosaur books—but not like this one! It is huge, with page-length articles on all sorts of dinosaur behavior. Perhaps its best feature, though, is the full-action illustrations, which pop right off the page. This one book is good for countless hours of browsing fun for even the most rabid dinosaur fan.

Anthony Horowitz. *Stormbreaker.* Alex Rider Adventures series. Philomel, 2001.

Alex Rider is a spy, but he's no James Bond. He's fourteen years old, and his cool gadgets come looking like yo-yos and zit cream. There's a bigger difference, though, and he knows what it is. "In the end," he tells himself, "the big difference between him and James Bond wasn't a question of age. It was a question of loyalty. In the old days, spies had done what they'd done because they loved their country, because they believed in what they were doing. But he'd never been given a choice. Nowadays, spies weren't employed. They were used" (p. 228). That makes Alex one unlikely spy, but when his uncle, the man who raised him, is killed on a mission for MI6, the British Secret Service, Alex finds himself in the family business, picking up where his uncle left off, trying to get to the bottom of a terrorist plot, and hoping to get out of it alive. It all revolves around a new type of computer that's being delivered to every school in England—a very generous gift. So why is MI6 so interested, and Alex's uncle so dead? Alex needs to find out before the clock strikes noon.

Richard Jennings. *The Great Whale of Kansas*. Houghton Mifflin, 2001.

> "I was well on my way to having what I've always wanted," I told him. "A pond of my very own. But now that there's the possibility of getting something I never even thought of having before, I find that I want it, instead. Is this wrong?"
>
> Phil said nothing, which is his customary response. (pp. 19–20)

(Because, of course, Phil is a duck.)

Alternate Booktalk

"Facts are funny things. No matter how many you discover, there are always more you know you should have found . . . On any given day, the facts we know can be replaced by those we don't. Honestly, it wouldn't surprise me if after we're dead, we found out we didn't know anything at all" (p. 137). Fact: Melville, Kansas, is the geographic center of the United States. Fact: Higly Park, in Melville, Kansas, is a very quiet place. Fact: there were no whales in the age of dinosaurs. And two of those three facts are about to change in *The Great Whale of Kansas*, by Richard Jennings.

Gordon Korman. *The Chicken Doesn't Skate*. Scholastic, 1996.

What is a chicken? Some say it is a pet, others see it as a meal with feathers, still others see it as a wondrous work of nature, but there are some who believe a chicken is really the secret weapon of the South Middle School Rangers hockey team! How can a chicken win a hockey championship? Find out in *The Chicken Doesn't Skate*, by Gordon Korman.

Gordon Korman. *Schooled*. Hyperion, 2007.

Cap is the last of the hippies, a teenage boy living with just his tie-dye-wearing grandmother on a nearly defunct commune. He eats what he grows, he wears what he makes, he doesn't watch TV, he doesn't believe in private property, and modern society cannot put up with such insanity. So when his grandmother is suddenly taken out of the picture, Cap is grabbed and sentenced to a punitive institution: public school! Cap, though, is tougher than he looks, and he is not the only one who is about to get *Schooled*.

Mike Lupica. *The Big Field*. Penguin, 2008.

> The lefty tried to get him to chase a dinky pitch, off the outside corner by a foot. Hutch took it for ball one. Then the kid basically threw him the same pitch again, one that was still outside, though not by as much.

The ump called it a strike.

"Hey ump," Mr. Cullen called down from the first base coach's box. "That pitch was closer to me than to my kid."

The ump was out from behind the plate in a shot. "Zip it, coach. *Now.*"

Mr. Cullen wasn't quite ready to let it go. "Just making an observation."

"Keep your observations to yourself the rest of the way."

"Sorry to have mentioned it," Mr. Cullen said, walking back towards first.

Sometimes he'd get into it with an umpire, even for an exchange as brief as that one had been, just to get a pitcher out of his rhythm. Hutch just stayed where he was, deep breathing, the bat resting on his shoulder, trying to think along with the pitcher. The lefty tried to go away again.

This one really did catch part of the plate. Or would have if Hutch, going the other way with it, hadn't laid all over it.

Hutch hadn't been sure of his first home run of the night, not until he saw that the outfielders had stopped running.

He was sure about this one.

He still ran hard to first, because that was the way you were supposed to play ball.

But this baby was gone.

Gone, baby, gone.

This time he saw the whole thing: The Yankees right fielder stopping dead in his tracks, dropping to one knee as the ball left the yard.

By the time Hutch rounded second base, he didn't feel like he was running at all.

More like he was floating.

The whole team was waiting for him at home plate, everybody jumping and pounding each other as Hutch rounded third. Hutch saw the guy with the Channel 12 television camera standing a few feet away, shooting the whole thing.

Then a TV camera was pointed straight at Hutch for the first time in his life.

Yeah.

Hutch was definitely floating. (pp. 45–47)

And that was just the first game of the tournament.

Chris Lynch. *Gold Dust.* HarperCollins, 2000.

[Hide the book behind your back.] Jim Rice and Fred Lynn came to the Red Sox together as rookies in 1975, but Napoleon Charlie Ellis noticed they were not treated quite the same by the Fenway fans, so he turned to his friend Richard and said, "'They clap for Fred Lynn even when he appears to have done something foolish.'"

Richard replied, "'They were applauding the *effort,* Napoleon, the hustle.'"

"And when he struck out, that took great effort?"

"Maybe." . . .

"He struck out, the same as Jim Rice."

"Like I told you, it happens—"

"But the people clapped madly for Mr. Lynn anyway. Not so much for Mr. Rice. . . . What does that mean, Richard?" (pp. 184–85)

So I'll ask you, what do you suppose made Fred Lynn so different from Jim Rice? Richard knows, he just doesn't want to think about it. Napoleon has to think about it, because he's different too. [Show the kids the cover of the book.]

Alternate Booktalk

I stand in there, scratching hard into the frozen dirt of the petrified batter's box with my spikes. Butchie keeps grinning, leans back, and back and back, then comes over the top, and over and over, and finally reaches his perfect release point and lets go of the first pitch of the 1975 baseball season.

It whistles. It is such a beautiful thing, the sound of it, the East-West spin—which I can pick up easily in the superior clarity of winter's air—that I am almost too excited to react properly to the pitch until . . .

I drop to the ground, flopping hard on my back an instant before the ball nails me in the head.

"If you can't stand the heat . . ." Butchie says, blowing warm steaming air through his pitching hand.

Could've told you he was going to do that.

I do love this game. (pp. 8–9)

Kadir Nelson. *We Are the Ship: The Story of Negro League Baseball.* Jump at the Sun, 2008.

The Negro Leagues were tough. The first catcher to wear shin guards was from the Negro Leagues; he got sick of leaving the field on crutches after getting his legs ripped open by a runner's spikes, so he strapped a couple of barrel staves to his shins. The first batting helmet was an old miner's helmet that a Negro League batter wore because the pitchers threw so many spitballs, shine balls, cut balls, and emery balls that you never knew where a pitch was going to go. Of course off the field was tougher. Negro League players had to deal with the Ku Klux Klan. Some teams traveled to games in the back of pickup trucks because they couldn't afford railroad passes, and some teams played as many as four games a day just to make enough money to live on. Some of the best players in the world never got a chance to play in the big leagues. This is their story, in words and paintings, in legend and history, in full color, of the black and the white of baseball, of how the Negro Leagues gave players a chance to play ball, how their success launched some of the great players into the major leagues, and how that success spelled the end of the Negro Leagues.

Richard Peck. *The Teacher's Funeral: A Comedy in Three Acts.* **Dial, 2004.**

When your school has only one room and one teacher, and the teacher dies just days before school starts, then you might expect to be free from school for the year. Russell thought that, until his older sister reached into the coffin of his former teacher and pried the pointer she carried from her cold, dead fingers. This will be a school year to remember.

Rodman Philbrick. *The Young Man and the Sea.* **Blue Sky, 2004.**

I love action and adventure stories, and to me, the best part is the beginning of the journey. What makes someone set off on an adventure? Especially if they have to set off on their own? What does it take to take that first step, or turn the key in the ignition, or put the oars into the water? What do you have to leave behind? Home, family, friends, food, warmth, comfort, safety? The first step of an adventure takes more courage than all the others.

Let me share the first step of Samuel "Skiff" Beaman's journey:

> There it is, right at my fingertips. My father's harpoon. . . . I lift it off the pegs, expecting heavy, but the harpoon is light. Long and light and balanced where you hold it. The surprise of that makes me dizzy. . . . When I'm breathing again I worry some more about Mr. Woodwell. What'll he say if he finds me taking his harpoon? What'll I say back? Can't think of nothing that makes it right, but that don't stop me doing it. I been over it in my own head and there's no way around it. . . . I got to head out tonight and be there when the sun comes up, ready to strike the first big fish that rises. Need a harpoon for that, no two ways about it. . . . I scurry down the bank to where my skiff is waiting. The harpoon is longer than the boat. . . . Big old harpoon is meant to be used, ain't it? . . . Once I'm out on the creek I stop worrying about Mr. Woodwell and start thinking about the giant fish. The big bluefin. I can almost hear it talking. Sassing me like a bully in the schoolyard. *Come and get me, lobster boy. Come and get me if you dare.* (pp. 116–18)

Darren Shan. *Cirque Du Freak.* **Cirque Du Freak: The Saga of Darren Shan series. Little Brown, 2001.**

If you get frightened easily by creepy-crawly things, feel free to cover your ears while I talk about this next book. If you like that sort of thing, try to picture the following scene vividly in your mind:

> The goat gave a leap when the spider landed and bleated loudly. Madam Octa took no notice . . . she bared her fangs and sunk them deep into the goat's neck! The goat shivered and went totally still. It was dead.

"You will be safe now," Mr. Crepsley said, "But please, do not make any loud noises, because if you do, she might come after me."

I don't know if Mr. Crepsley was really scared, or if it was part of the act, but he looked frightened. He wiped the sleeve of his right arm over his forehead, then placed the flute back in his mouth and whistled a strange little tune.

Madam Octa cocked her head, then appeared to nod. She crawled across the table until she was in front of Mr. Crepsley. He lowered his right hand and she crept up his arm. The thought of those long hairy legs creeping along his flesh made me sweat all over. And I liked spiders!

People who were afraid of them must have been nervously chewing the insides of their cheeks to pieces. (pp. 78–80)

And that's just one of the acts in the *Cirque Du Freak*!

Lemony Snicket. *The Bad Beginning*. A Series of Unfortunate Events series. HarperCollins, 1999.

Don't you just hate happy endings? Don't you just hate it when the bad guy always loses? Don't you just hate stories about perfect little children . . . living with their perfect little parents . . . in a perfect little town . . . in their perfect little house . . . with their perfect little dog? Well, if you do, then you may be one of the special few to enjoy a Series of Unfortunate Events. In book 1 alone, three perfect children run into a disastrous fire; a greedy, mean count; ugly clothing; and cold oatmeal for breakfast. And it only gets worse!

Lemony Snicket. *The Reptile Room*. A Series of Unfortunate Events series. HarperCollins, 1999.

With a flourish he swooped the cloth off the cage. Inside was a large black snake, as dark as a coal mine and as thick as a sewer pipe, looking right at the orphans with shiny green eyes. With the cloth off its cage, the snake began to uncoil itself and slither around his home.

"What's it called?" Violet asked.

"The Incredibly Deadly Viper," Uncle Monte replied, and at that moment something happened which I'm sure will interest you. With one flick of its tail, the snake unlatched the door of its cage and slithered out onto the table, and before Uncle Monty or any of the Baudelaire orphans could say anything, it opened its mouth and . . .

[Stop here and wait for loud objections. If you get enough of them, finish the sentence.]

. . . before Uncle Monty or any of the Baudelaire orphans could say anything, it opened its mouth and bit Sunny right on the chin. (p. 26)

To find out what happens next, you will have to read *The Reptile Room,* by Lemony Snicket.

Jerry Spinelli. *Loser.* **Joanna Cotler, 2002.**

How do I present this book to you? The title itself is a word we adults don't want you to use. But what if the word didn't matter? What if it didn't matter that you run with arms and legs flailing wildly and still you don't go anywhere? What if it didn't matter that you love school so much you show up on Saturday? What if you could wear a four-foot giraffe hat for the pure joy of wearing a four-foot giraffe hat? What if it was OK to be a loser? Wouldn't it be fun? And wouldn't it be great to know someone who could do all those goofy things, and a hundred more, and be just as happy as can be?

Jerry Spinelli. *Maniac Magee.* **Little, Brown, 1990.**

> At last McNab was back on the mound, fingering the ball in his glove, a demon's gleam in his eye. He wound up, fired, the ball headed for the plate, and—what's this?—a legball?—it's got legs—long legs pinwheeling toward the plate. It wasn't a ball at all, it was a frog, and McNab was on the mound cackling away, and the kid at the plate was bug-eyed. He'd never—*nobody'd* ever—tried to hit a fast*frog* before.
>
> So what did the kid do? He *bunted* it . . . laid down a perfect bunt in front of the plate, third-base side, and he took off for first. He was halfway to second before McNab jolted himself into action. The kid was trying for an inside-the-park home-run bunt—the rarest feat in baseball.
>
> So McNab lumbered off the mound after the frog, which was now hopping down the third-base line. As a matter of fact, it was so close to the line that McNab had a brilliant idea—just herd the frog across the line and it would be a foul ball (or frog). But the frog, instead of taking a left turn at the shoe, jumped over it and hopped on toward third base. He was heading for the green fields of left, and the runt kid was chucking dust for third.
>
> Only one hope now—McNab had to grab the frog and tag the runner out. But now the frog shot through his legs, over to the mound, and now toward shortstop and now toward second, and the kid was rounding third and digging for home and—unbefroggable!—the "ball" was heading back home too! The ball, the batter, the pitcher all racing for home plate, and it was the batter, the new kid out of nowhere, who crossed the plate first . . .
>
> And that's how Jeffrey Magee knocked the world's first frogball for a four-bagger. (pp. 25–27)

You may know "Jeffrey Magee" better as "Maniac Magee," from the book with the same title, by Jerry Spinelli.

Todd Strasser. *Help! I'm Trapped in My Lunch Lady's Body.* **Help! I'm Trapped . . . series. Scholastic, 1999.**

> My friends and I in the lunch lady bodies trudged back toward the kitchen.
>
> I couldn't believe it! "You guys really want to be lunch ladies for the rest of your lives?"
>
> "There are worse things," said Andy in April's body.
>
> "Like what?" I asked in May's body.
>
> . . . and the survey says . . .
>
> #3 Armpit sniffer in a deodorant factory
>
> #2 Athlete's foot medicine tester
>
> And the #1 job that is worse than lunch lady . . . The guy with the shovel who walks behind the elephants at the circus. (p. 49)

Brad Strickland. *The Whistle, the Grave, and the Ghost.* **Lewis Barnavelt series. Dial, 2003.**

A big-time mystery, with all the ingredients:

A silver whistle that seems to appear and disappear of its own accord . . .

Two boys with an unexplainable illness . . .

A strange and beautiful woman who steps from the shadows, then is gone . . .

Voices in the dark . . .

Messages that no one can decipher . . .

And a grave in the woods that shouldn't be there.

Unravel it all with the best-known detective who is still too young to drive, Lewis Barnavelt.

Michael Sullivan. *The Sapphire Knight.* **The Bard series. PublishingWorks, 2009.**

A young traveler sits beside a fire on an open heath and hears a most amazing tale from a broken and disfigured old man, a tale of sorcery and battle between the light of a great white castle and the dark green wood, between the White Lady and the Green Queen. Caught between two great powers, a young knight must discover truth and his own courage to defend that truth. But is it just an idle tale of a lying old man, or is it the true history of the Sapphire Knight?

Michael Teitelbaum. *The Scary States of America.* **Delacorte, 2007.**

Fifty states, fifty stories of ghosts, aliens, supernatural phenomenon, and things that go bump in the night. Geography goes *X-Files* in *The Scary States of America.*

Timothy Tocher. *Chief Sunrise, John McGraw, and Me.* **Cricket, 2004.**

Baseball fans in the crowd? What would you do to get a shot at the big leagues? Would you jump from a moving train? Would you share living quarters with a horse? Guys, would you play baseball in a skirt? Would you change your name and pretend to be someone you are not?

Hank Cobb and Chief Sunrise have to do all this and more to get a chance to try out before the greatest big-league manager in history in *Chief Sunrise, John McGraw, and Me.*

Wendelin Van Draanen. *Swear to Howdy.* **Knopf, 2003.**

> While Sissy's handing the cokes over to mama and dad, Joey's face is all frantic, trying to tell me something.
>
> "What?" I whispered.
>
> He just kept twitching at the face.
>
> "What?" I asked again, and then it clicked. He hadn't put bugs in just Sissy and Amanda Jane's drinks. He'd put them in all the cups. My eyes shot back and forth. From my parents to my sister. From my parents to my sister. And when I was sure no one was looking, I mouthed, "Bugs?"
>
> He nodded.
>
> I whispered, "Why?"
>
> "Didn't want 'em to go to waste!"
>
> . . . We were almost out of the park when the screaming started.
>
> (pp. 17–19)

David Ward. *Escape the Mask.* **The Grassland Trilogy series. Amulet, 2008.**

Not all fantasy involves mythological creatures and magic, only a world based on "What if?" What if you grew up a slave, living in caves and driven to work each day of your young life by silent warriors, forced to labor until you came of age, when you were separated from all you knew and disappeared forever? If you lived that way, the only thing more frightening than your closed little world would be a door to the unknown. When that door opens, once in all of time, do you step out into what you know only as "Outside"?

Chris Woodford and Jon Woodcock. *Cool Stuff 2.0 and How It Works.* **Dorling Kindersley, 2007.**

From how a jackhammer or a laser works to skateboard simulators to robots that can read and react to human emotions—and to a mechanical cat that farts air freshener—here is the inside scoop, in full color.

CHAPTER 8

BOOKTALKS FOR HIGH SCHOOL BOYS

Isabel Allende. *City of the Beasts.* **Rayo, 2002.**

A story of survival in the jungle. From anaconda attacks to finding food in the Amazon, fifteen-year-old Alex Cold is way out of his element. Specifically, he's thousands of miles from Southern California, with only his cold and very odd grandmother Kate for family. But the Amazon has many secrets, people who can fade into the mist, creatures that kill without being seen, and magic that appears in the strangest places. But strangest and most magical of all the wonders of the jungle is the honey-colored girl Nadia, who seems to be as much a part of the jungle as she is a human being. Alex will need all her help and strength he doesn't even know he has if he is going to escape the *City of the Beasts.*

Terence Blacker. *Boy 2 Girl.* **Farrar, Strauss, and Giroux, 2005.**

When an American girl shows up at a school in London, England, you might expect her to call football "soccer" and to have some weird ideas about food and clothes and music. But you don't expect her to beat up the school bully, waltz into the boys' bathroom, and get arrested in a football (or soccer) riot. Her English teacher thinks she's secretly shy and insecure. The school Romeo thinks she's irresistible and doesn't know why. Her gangster father thinks he only has a son. Who's right? Who's wrong? And who is just really confused?

Joseph Bruchac. *Bearwalker.* **HarperCollins, 2007.**

A story of survival and terror in the woods of New York State from one of the great storytellers, orally and in print, of our generation.

Philip Caveney. *Sebastian Darke: Prince of Pirates.* **Delacorte, 2009.**

Sebastian Darke is back in another humorous and epic adventure with his pint-size warrior buddy and his morose talking "buffalope." This time, he is trading in his jester's cap for a sword and taking on huge snakes, enchantresses, sea monsters, and bloodthirsty pirates. Anchors aweigh with Philip Caveney's *Sebastian Darke: Prince of Pirates.*

Daniel Defoe. *Robinson Crusoe.* **Great Illustrated Classics. Abdo and Daughters, 2002.**

Your ship is wrecked, killing all your companions. Is God punishing you? You alone survive. Is God protecting you? Twenty years marooned on an island you thought was deserted, but now you discover you are not alone. Do you want to know who is waiting for you on the other side of the island? Ask Robinson Crusoe.

Carl Deuker. *Gym Candy.* **Houghton Mifflin, 2007.**

The problem with sports is that no matter how good you are, it seems like there is always someone better. And the better you are, the more that hurts. There is a phrase they use in football: "One man to beat." If you had one man to beat to fulfill your lifelong dream, how far would you go to beat him? With the steroid scandal in baseball fresh on everyone's mind, *Gym Candy* is a story that takes an exceptionally raw look at the temptation to do anything to be the best. Most disturbingly, this isn't about a multimillionaire athlete trying to buy one more year, one more record; this is about a normal American teenager. Hold tight; this one hits hard.

Kathleen Duey. *Skin Hunger.* **A Resurrection of Magic series. Atheneum, 2007.**

Can the power of magic save a people from an oppressive king? Or do you need a powerful king to save you from oppressive magicians? Kathleen Duey winds together two stories, hundreds of years apart, on opposite sides of an epic battle, and tied together by an eerie secret. Have the hunters become the hunted? And when the tables turn, what will be the revenge? The story of a Resurrection of Magic begins with *Skin Hunger.*

David Elliott. *Jeremy Cabbage and the Living Museum of Human Oddballs and Quadruped Delights.* **Knopf, 2008.**

David Elliott's book is for those kids who just haven't connected with anything since Lemony Snicket's Series of Unfortunate Events. It's smart and funny and has a smart pig; what more do you want?

Samantha Ettus. *The Experts' Guide to 100 Things Everyone Should Know.* **Clarkson Potter, 2004.**

How would you like to have Donald Trump tell you how to negotiate in two or three pages? Or have Howie Mandel teach you how to tell a joke? Or Debbie Fields (Mrs. Fields!) teach you how to make cookies? Or Bob Vila teach you how to paint a room? This book has a NASCAR driver telling you how to change your oil, a dating expert telling you how to ask someone out, and chef Bobby Flay giving you a crash course in how to barbeque.

D. L. Garfinkle. *Storky: How I Lost My Nickname and Won the Girl.* **Putnam, 2005.**

From the electronic journal of Michael "Storky" Pomerantz, high school freshman:

THINGS TO DO WITHOUT A TV
1. Read a book.
2. Memorize Scrabble words.
3. Stare at Victoria's Secret catalog again.
4. Watch TV at Nate's.
5. Bike to Circuit City and watch TV there. (p. 74)

Should I ask Sydney to the Spring Fling?

CONS
1. At this point in my pathetic life, the last thing I need is her turning me down.
2. I'm broke.
3. I still have bad memories of the Snowball.

PROS
1. At this point in my pathetic life, what I need is a date with Sydney Holland.
2. I could earn $8 an hour this weekend.
3. Maybe I could finally kiss a girl. (pp. 145–46)

WHAT I LEARNED FROM THE SNOWBALL
1. Don't go out with anyone on the rebound.
2. Make reservations for dinner.
3. If a pretty girl keeps pulling up her strapless dress, don't take your eyes off her. (p. 173)

Alison Goodman. *Eon: Dragoneye Reborn.* **Viking, 2008.**

There has been a recent trend toward fantasy based on the martial arts, from Jeff Stone's Five Ancestors to Lian Hearn's Tales of the Otori series.

Alison Goodman has the latest entrant, with *Eon: Dragoneye Reborn*. The power of twelve dragons stands behind the empire, and each dragon works through his appointed emissary and an apprentice. But the most powerful dragon of all has deserted the world for centuries until the most unlikely of apprentices is called. There's plenty of swordplay and powerful magic in this epic fantasy based on karate and Chinese mythology.

David Grann. *The Lost City of Z: A Tale of Deadly Obsession in the Amazon.* **Doubleday, 2009.**

This nonfiction account covers one hundred years of fateful, and even fatal, expeditions into the heart of the Amazon region. It is part adventure tale, part horror story, part ecological treatise, all wrapped up in some amazing storytelling. This is Bill Bryson with teeth! It is a tropical *Into Thin Air.* Journalist David Grann follows in the footsteps of some of the greatest explorers ever into a land that even the great explorers could not conquer to try to solve a mystery as old as history in the New World. He goes in search of the golden city of El Dorado.

John Grisham. *Playing for Pizza.* **Doubleday, 2007.**

You've heard of football players getting knocked out? Well, Rick Dockery got knocked out, knocked out of the game, knocked out of the NFL, knocked out of America, and knocked out of the Western Hemisphere. He got knocked so hard he landed in Italy. Name one great football player from Italy. My point exactly. *Playing for Pizza* follows the final demise of the career of a once-promising professional quarterback. After blowing the biggest lead in history, he must escape murderous fans and find somewhere to play football (because not playing football is not an option) where nobody watches the NFL. How far will he go to play the game he loves? You have no idea!

Lian Hearn. *The Sword of the Warrior.* **Tales of the Otori series. Firebird, 2002.**

Otori Takeo is bound by faith to the Hidden, a secretive religious group that is being hunted to extinction; by honor to the Otori, a proud warrior clan; and by blood to the Tribe, a mystical guild of spies and assassins. Everyone wants a piece of Takeo, and if they can't have it, they want him dead. He will need every weapon he has, both in his hands and in his head, if he is going to survive in this fantasy realm set in feudal Japan.

Matsuri Hino. *Vampire Knight.* **Shojo Beat, 2007–.**

Cross Academy is where opposites meet, where paths cross. The day class crosses paths with the night class at dawn and twilight, when the two halves of the school switch places, one half to their dorms and the other to their classes. The students in the night class are all tall, beautiful, and pale, and they don't go out during the day. Why? Because they are all vampires. The school is a fragile attempt to prove that vampires and humans can coexist and end their centuries-old war. But can they live together? None of the day class knows the secret except two class protectors, who keep watch. One was saved by a vampire as a child; the other was attacked by one as a child. These opposites stand where two worlds meet at Cross Academy in *Vampire Knight*, the manga by Matsuri Hino.

Chris Humphreys. *The Fetch*. The Runestone Saga series. Knopf, 2006.

Which would be more frightening? Meeting your distant ancestor on the deck of a Viking ship, meeting your grandfather—dead for forty years—in a cabin lost in the woods of Norway, or meeting yourself coming out of your school just as you are going in? Time melts and the dead walk in this part horror, part fantasy based on Norse mythology. It is the Runestone Saga, by Chris Humphreys.

Satomi Ikezawa. *Othello*. Del Rey, 2004–.

Yaya Higuchi is shy, quiet, and just wants to be liked. Yeah, she's a pushover. And people push her and push her. But don't push her too far, because her mysterious friend Nana, hip, confident, and with a terrific spin kick, always seems to show up just when Yaya is being pushed to the edge. Friends and foes alike are mystified, but Yaya herself never sees her protector; her memory has a way of blanking out every time Nana appears. Othello, black and white, opposites, flip sides of the same coin. What is Nana's secret?

A. M. Jenkins. *Night Road*. HarperTeen, 2008.

A thoroughly modern and human vampire story. They prowl the night, seeking out the lonely in anonymous bars, puncturing their necks and drinking their life's blood, then moving on to the next feed. Does that make them bad people?

Dean Koontz and Queenie Chan. *In Odd We Trust*. Ballantine, 2008.

Odd Thomas may be the most endearing character ever created by Dean Koontz, the king of creep. This nineteen-year-old fry cook makes the best pancakes, hangs out with a kick-ass girlfriend named Stormy, and drives around town with Elvis. Oh yeah, did I mention? He can see the dead. In this first graphic novel in the Odd Thomas saga, he has to reach out to one brutally murdered boy to help stop the next tragedy, but the bad guy seems more than half a ghost himself. Something strange and evil is at work, and, of course, Dean Koontz is behind it all.

Gordon Korman. *No More Dead Dogs.* **Hyperion, 2002.**

If you have been in school for at least three days, you know the deal. A teacher hands you a book, and on page 1, you are introduced to a boy and his dog. What's going to happen?

Right. The dog's gonna die.

Wallace Wallace knows this, too, but Wallace Wallace has a little character flaw: he cannot tell a lie. So when his English teacher assigns a book report on *Old Shep, My Pal*, Wallace Wallace says it is just one more dumb dead dog book. But *Old Shep, My Pal* is the teacher's favorite book, and the teacher is also the director of the school play: you guessed it, *Old Shep, My Pal*. How will he show Wallace Wallace the true beauty of this heart-wrenching story? He makes Wallace Wallace skip football practice and sit in on rehearsals until Wallace Wallace sees the light, and the battle of nerves is on.

But, you know, if you complain about something long enough, people expect you to fix it. And that is how Wallace Wallace becomes the new director of *Old Shep, My Pal*, and now he, his buddies, the drama club, and the football team, along with an Eastern European pizza delivery boy on a moped, must guarantee that there are *no more dead dogs!* In *No More Dead Dogs*, by Gordon Korman.

Michael Lewis. *The Blind Side: Evolution of a Game.* **Norton, 2007.**

Michael Oher went from an unknown street kid in Memphis to one of the hottest prospects in the NFL draft. Michael Lewis not only tells this young man's incredible true story but puts it in the context of the evolving game of professional football, the lurid world of big-time college football, race relations, and economic realities. The story bounces from one perspective to another so quickly that the author makes narrative nonfiction writing look like a music video, with astonishing results. The book is beyond gripping, and the best sports book yet for those teenage boys who dream of playing professional football or just being able to talk ball with their dads.

Alfred C. Martino. *Pinned.* **Harcourt, 2005.**

Two young men on a collision course . . .

They have a lot in common. They are high school wrestlers, and they are good; possibly they are the best. They both have sacrificed more than most of us can imagine. Hours of practice every day is just the beginning—the running, the weights, the workouts. They have barely eaten in months; they measure out the water they drink drop by drop. Everything and everyone in their lives have taken second place so they won't have to.

They are on a collision course . . .

But they are different, too. One lives in a grand house; the other in a house that is falling down. One has a proud team to wrestle for; the other wrestles for himself. One wrestles to escape his home life for a few precious hours; the other to escape his life forever.

But they always have one thing in common: they are determined to be the best, and there can be only one best.

So, they are on a collision course, in Alfred C. Martino's *Pinned.*

Mitsukazu Mihara. *Haunted House.* **TokyoPop, 2006.**

Oh, you think your family's weird? Try living with *The Addams Family* meets *Tales from the Crypt.* Try having parents who met at a horror film and fell in love at first sight. Try living with twin sisters who paint you all over with corpse makeup while you sleep. And worse, try bringing a girl home to meet the family! Sabato has tried it sixty-six times and been dumped immediately by sixty-six different girls. How can you escape the haunted house, when the haunted house is what you call home? It's comedy; it's horror; it's manga; it's *Haunted House,* by Mitsukazu Mihara.

Christopher Moore. *A Dirty Job.* **William Morrow, 2006.**

Charlie is a timid little lovable loser who runs a secondhand shop in San Francisco until his life becomes impossibly great. The perfect woman actually agrees to marry him, and they have a beautiful little baby girl. Charlie wants nothing else but for everything to stay the way it is. Of course, everything but that happens. His wife dies suddenly, and a huge black man wearing a lime green suit appears out of nowhere beside her deathbed; steals her favorite CD; and calmly informs Charlie that he is the next Grim Reaper and hands him the *Big Book of Death.* Charlie's young daughter's first words kill a man. Charlie is being hunted by huge, man-size ravens, and two hell hounds come to his house and decide to become his pets. I guess death is a dirty little job, but someone's got to do it.

Walter Dean Myers. *Monster.* **Amistad, 1999.**

Something terrible happens three days before Christmas in a drugstore in Harlem. One man is shot and killed, and one young man of sixteen is now in jail and on trial for his life. What does it feel like to be locked up and always afraid, too afraid to talk, to sleep, even to cry? How does it feel to hear someone call you a monster? And how does it feel to wonder if you might actually be a monster? Steve Harmon tells his own story in his own words and through the lens of a movie camera that is always running in his own mind. This is not a happy little story. Sometimes a story is more real than what you are likely to see on the news, and *Monster,* by Walter Dean Myers, is one of those stories.

Walter Dean Myers. *Sunrise over Fallujah.* **Scholastic, 2008.**

> I didn't feel anything special as we were waved into line to cross from Kuwait into Iraq. I remembered an orientation booklet the navy had passed around talking about how Iraq was known as the cradle of civilization. We were headed into Babylon and we were excited.
>
> "Yo Birdy!" Marla's voice crackled in the intercom.
>
> "What?"
>
> "Check out that line of green on your left," she said.
>
> Me and Jonesy looked over and saw some civilians laying something in a neat line on the ground. "What is it?" Jonesy asked.
>
> "Body bags," Marla said. "Welcome to Iraq." (p. 91)

Blake Nelson. *Gender Blender.* **Delacorte, 2006.**

> "This is really happening," she murmured. "I'm too strong for my own good. I'm acting like a complete idiot. And I smell like somebody's crotch. Oh my God, I'm totally a boy!" (p. 43)

James Patterson. *School's Out—Forever.* **Maximum Ride series. Warner, 2006.**

Six teenage mutant freaks are on the run, or on the wing, in this James Patterson sci-fi thriller series. Everyone dreams of being able to fly, to soar like birds into the open skies. But Maximum Ride and her flock of half-human, half-bird experiments grew up in cages. They may be free now, but white-coated scientists, FBI agents, and a pack of mutant half-wolf hunters are determined to clip their wings. While the bird-kids are discovering new dangers, they are also discovering new powers, and it is all rising toward a final battle for the fate of the world in *School's Out—Forever.*

Gary Paulsen. *The Car.* **Harcourt Brace, 1994.**

Terry is fourteen when his parents have a huge fight. Each one storms out, assuming the other will stay and take care of Terry. They aren't coming back. Now Terry has a house, a put-together roadster in the garage, and a choice. Stay or go? What would you do?

Terry Pratchett. *Thud!* **Discworld series. HarperCollins, 2005.**

The city of Ankh-Morpork is ready to explode. All right, the city of Ankh-Morpork is always ready to explode. After all, this is a place where the assassins have their own guild, there are golems working in the post office, and the local reporter is a vampire. But the trolls and the dwarfs are drawing up battle lines, ready to refight a thousand-year-old battle that has become a popular board game. And when the great and holy leader of the dwarfs is found dead from a blow to the head, with a troll club lying beside him, the news hits the city with a loud *thud!*

Graham Salisbury. *Night of the Howling Dogs.* **Wendy Lamb, 2007.**

> We're dead, I thought as I heard the ocean churning toward us. Rumbling in, slow at first, then rising up, faster and faster.
>
> "Pop!" Mike shouted, trying to run toward the coconut grove. He never made it.
>
> Water rushed in. It grabbed my ankles, swirled around them, and rose higher. I tried to slog inland, but there was nowhere to go. Louie flashed his light out at the mountain of white water boiling toward us as the earth continued to sink, taking us down with it. He whipped the light back toward the cliff. Boulders flashed in the beam, tumbling down. In the eerie light, two huge monsters bounced over our shelter, crushing it, then rolled on to vanish in the oncoming sea.
>
> "Louie!" I howled. The sea was bearing down on us like a garbage truck. He whipped the light back.
>
> The wall of water came at us head-on, a mountain in the puny beam of light. We stumbled back, falling over rocks we couldn't see. Going down, struggling to stand. Louie heaved Casey up onto his shoulders and staggered inland. He tried to hang on to the flashlight, but it was lost in the ocean rushing around our waists. The light glowed underwater and went out as it sank.
>
> The ocean knocked me off my feet. I flailed inland, my glasses tight in my fist. I would never let them go, no matter what. I gasped a last breath . . . and went under. (pp. 113–14)

Ken Scholes. *Lamentation.* **Tor, 2009.**

In a postapocalyptic world, centuries after the folly of man has pushed civilization to the brink, the world has been reordered and brought together again, until an ancient evil is recalled to destroy the center of this emerging civilization. Now all powers strive, in ways both forthright and subtle, to fill the void and dominate what is left over. At the center of the storm is a warrior of great destiny, a boy caught in the whirlwind, a woman who is being played like a piece on a board, and a long-dead leader who has returned to this turbulent world in hopes of saving it. Passion, power, ambition, and enlightenment mix in a fast-paced tale of a world that yet may be.

Neal Schusterman. *Unwind.* **Simon and Schuster, 2007.**

Many years from now, our country has solved the abortion controversy. We don't abort babies; we wait until they are teenagers and abort them then! It makes sense, doesn't it? We have no idea of the potential of an unborn child, but by the time that child becomes a teenager, we have a pretty good idea. And think of all the good you can do with all those organs, blood, and tissue. Sound good? Dystopias usually do. But when all of society agrees that an evil is right, who will have the courage to stand up against it? If teenagers are being victimized, then they have to do it, and quickly in Neal Schusterman's *Unwind*.

William Shakespeare. Illustrated by Sonia Leong. *Romeo and Juliet***. Manga Shakespeare series. Amulet, 2007.**

Why don't kids understand Shakespeare when they read his works? Because Shakespeare wrote plays, and plays are meant to be seen, not read. Now, kids can read Shakespeare, his actual words, and see the story unfold. In the first of the Manga Shakespeare series, Romeo and Juliet are no old Italians in tights; they are young and hip kids in modern-day Tokyo. And the Japanese have better swords.

Darren Shan. *Slawter.* **The Demonata series. Little, Brown, 2006.**

> "I've always wanted to eat human flesh. I mean, it's not an obsession or anything. I wouldn't want to go out of my way to kill, skin, and cook somebody. But I've always been curious, wondered what it would taste like. So, when the opportunity dropped into my lap, yeah, I took it. Does that make me a bad person? I don't think so. At least, not much badder than—"
> "Worse than," Bill-E interrupts.
> "*Worse!*" Emmet winces. "I keep tripping on that."
> . . . I feel sorry for Emmet, watching him struggle to learn his lines. (p. 61)

It's a movie, just a movie. A movie about horrible demons massacring people. It's being filmed on a secret set, way off in the desert, where no one can see, where no one can interfere, where no one can leave. And now they have brought in the experts, a man and a boy who have faced demons, real demons, faced them, fought them, and defeated the demon master who vowed he would kill them horribly if he ever got them alone . . .

It's book 3 in the Demonata series, by Darren Shan.

Ken Silverstein. *The Radioactive Boy Scout: The True Story of a Boy and His Backyard Nuclear Reactor.* **Random House, 2004.**

He built what? He built it where? How? Didn't anybody notice? How can an ordinary kid working in a potting shed do something that generations of scientists with their PhDs and fancy laboratories have failed to do? How did he even think to try? This one is just too amazing to miss.

David Skuy. *Off the Crossbar.* **Writer's Collective, 2006.**

You know those sports guys who are always saying things like, "Hockey is like life . . ."? Do you know why they say things like that? Because hockey is like life. Hockey teaches us that little things can make a big difference. One player or one friend, one shift on the ice, or one more day with your dad. One decision can change a game or change your life, and one inch either way can send a puck into the net or off the crossbar. Little things do count, on the ice and in life, in *Off the Crossbar,* by David Skuy.

Roland Smith. *Elephant Run.* Hyperion, 2007.

One thing about war: it makes it hard to decide who to trust. Who are the bad guys, and who are the good guys? The Burmese in World War II had to decide who was worse—the colonizing English or the invading Japanese. On a plantation in Burma, the English overseers had to decide who to trust—the simpering house servants or the strong-willed field hands. And for one English boy trapped behind enemy lines, do you trust the dominant bull elephant that can crush your enemies beneath his feet or just as easily crush you? Everyone has to choose sides when war breaks out in Roland Smith's *Elephant Run.*

Sue Stauffacher. *Who Is He?* Wireman series. Sue Stauffacher, 2005.

Who needs adventure when just getting to, through, and from school is a life-and-death struggle? Andre is prey in the urban jungle until a huge and reclusive stranger puts his mark on him. Hero or phantom? Comic-book character or real-life hero? In a world this dark, who can tell the difference?

Rebecca Stead. *First Light.* Wendy Lamb, 2007.

For those who loved *The City of Ember,* here is another alternate-history sci-fi about a lost culture, cut off from the rest of the world, taking its own path. How would your life be different if you lived it entirely under the polar ice?

Todd Strasser. *Boot Camp.* Simon and Schuster, 2007.

Garrett was kidnapped, but his parents aren't worried; they paid to have it done. Two bounty hunters grabbed him, handcuffed him, threw him in the back of a car, and drove him to a place that is technically a school, but it looks like a prison, and it's run like a sadistic U.S. Marine base, all because he skipped a few classes, smoked a little, and, oh yeah, there was that stuff he did with his teacher. Did Garrett think that was enough to send him to a place where he was screamed at, punished, and put in solitary confinement? Actually, it doesn't matter what Garrett thinks anymore. His captors have complete power over him. All that matters is staying out of trouble, staying out of the guards' way, and staying alive long enough to get out of *Boot Camp.*

Todd Strasser. *Give a Boy a Gun.* Simon Pulse, 2002.

This is the story of two high school boys who just don't fit in, not with the jocks or the preppies or the nerds or the freaks, so they spend a lot of time with each other, alone in a basement, playing violent video games. And the more isolated they get, the angrier they get, until the only way out they can find is to walk into their school one day wearing ski masks and carrying bags full of guns and explosives.

Now, my question for you is this: Which is a more frightening thought, that this book is about Columbine High School or that it could be about a thousand schools just like it?

Todd Strasser. *Slide or Die*. Drift X series. Simon Pulse, 2006.

Sometimes Kennin wondered if there could be a better sensation in life than the feeling of tires breaking loose. With a loud squeal of rubber and a cloud of white smoke, the GTO's tail whipped around in a 180-degree turn . . . Wheels still spinning and screaming, Kennin straightened the car out and took off down the mountain road, using a feint drift to set up the first curve. In the rearview mirror a pair of headlights popped into view, with a rack of red and blue flashing lights above . . .

Heeling and toeing while working the clutch, Kennin never let the GTO's tach drop under 4,500 rpm or its tires find traction. In the headlights a large boulder appeared, just inside the corner of the next turn. Kennin aimed the nose of the car toward it. Beside him in the passenger seat, Tito braced his hands against the dashboard and screamed.

Kennin couldn't blame his friend for freaking. Working the clutch with his left foot as he heeled and toed the accelerator and brake, he drifted the GTO past the boulder, the nose of the car missing the rock by inches . . .

The winding mountain road was mostly tight, dropping turns perfect for linking drift after drift. The police cars' sirens and lights grew fainter as they lost more and more ground braking for the turns. Meanwhile, Kennin was now right on *Slide or Die*'s tail.

"Hey! Watch it!" Once again Tito braced his hands against the dashboard. "Look out! You're gonna T-bone him!"

The two cars went into the next curve drifting side by side in a cloud of white smoke with barely inches separating them . . . Tires squealing and smoking, Kennin kept the GTO's tach above 4,000 rpm as he and Chris drifted through another set of turns . . . Chris put the nose of the 240 SX into the next curve, but he'd misjudged the grade . . . Kennin saw the opportunity to go wide, putting the rear tires briefly on the gravel shoulder; then he jumped back onto the pavement and angled into the next curve.

Only now Chris Craven in his 240 SX was behind him. (pp. 49–52)

Jonathan Stroud. *The Amulet of Samarkand*. The Bartimaeus Trilogy series. Miramax, 2003.

Nathaniel may be just a magician's apprentice, but he somehow manages to summon up the powerful djinni Bartimaeus, just what he needs to exact a little revenge on the even more powerful magician Simon Lovelace. But an unwilling djinni is a dangerous ally, and there are world-shaking power struggles going on that young Nathaniel knows nothing about. How far will he go for revenge? And who, in the end, will end up paying the price?

James L. Swanson. *Chasing Lincoln's Killer.* **Scholastic, 2009.**

John Wilkes Booth originally planned to kidnap Abraham Lincoln and demand a Union surrender as ransom. But when the war ended before he could carry out his plan, he simply walked through all security, shot the president of the United States, and escaped while the audience at Ford's Theatre wondered if all the commotion was just part of the play. Thus started the greatest manhunt in American history, a twelve-day chase for the greatest traitor since Benedict Arnold. But there was so much more to the story: plots and subplots, coconspirators, other victims, and ultimately, four bodies hanging from the gallows. Everyone knows about the scene in the theater box when the hero of the Civil War was assassinated; here, told in the words and the documents of the day, is the rest of the story.

Richard Uhlig. *Boy minus Girl.* **Knopf, 2008.**

This book has, of course, the one big necessity of a teen angst book for boys—the loser boy who has no chance at the girl of his dreams. But man, this guy really has no chance. He doesn't have the muscles, the money, the attitude, the cool car, the breasts . . . the breasts? Can you say barking up the wrong tree?

Will Weaver. *Defect.* **Farrar, Strauss, and Giroux, 2007.**

A wounded angel or freak of nature? Gift or deformity? Special or just special needs? Differences force people to make decisions about what is real in this sci-fi medical tale. Something to read when you finish James Patterson's Maximum Ride books.

Joss Whedon, Karl Moline, and Andy Owens. *Fray.* **Dark Horse Comics, 2003.**

For fans of *Buffy the Vampire Slayer,* here is a futuristic view of the Slayer legend. Thousands of years in the future, the demons have all been defeated, the Slayers have ceased to be called, and the watchers, with all their knowledge and no way to use it, have gone mad. But who are these "Lurks" that now prowl the darkness, preying on the underbelly of society? One girl, with powers she does not understand, must face the rising tide in *Fray,* by Karl Moline, Andy Owens, and Joss Whedon, the man who brought Buffy to life.

Stanley "Tookie" Williams. *Life in Prison.* **Chronicle, 2001.**

In 1971, at the age of seventeen, Stanley "Tookie" Williams cofounded the notorious Crips gang that set off the bloodiest gang war in American history, between the Crips and the Bloods. Ten years later, Williams was sent to death row at San Quentin prison for multiple murder. But his life didn't end there. He lives on in a real-life hell on earth. This is the true story of life in a maximum security prison. No whitewashing, no punches pulled. Williams doesn't want you to follow in his footsteps, so he tells you exactly where those footsteps lead in *Life in Prison.*

Jake Wizner. *Spanking Shakespeare.* **Random House, 2007.**

Teen angst. Boy angst. Jewish angst. Moaning about his pathetic life, snot, bowel movements, and subversive adolescent stunts. Plus there are the requisite alcoholic fathers, depressed mothers, and torturously indifferent girls—and a whole lot of great laughs, too.

Futaro Yamada and Masaki Segawa. *Basilisk.* **Del Rey, 2006–.**

A four-hundred-year feud between two tribes of ninja is held at bay by an imposed truce until rivals for the control of Japan decide not to waste their strength in a bloody war. Instead, each contender for the throne chooses a ninja clan to champion his cause. The top ten ninja from each clan are put on a list, and the aim of the game is to wipe out the other clan's ninja and cross their names off the list. Now the twenty greatest ninja in all of Japan are off on a deadly assassins' scavenger hunt with an emperor's throne as a prize in *Basilisk.*

CHAPTER 9

INDIRECT READERS' ADVISORY

What in the world does "indirect readers' advisory" mean? It means finding ways to connect readers with books even when you are not there. It means posters and handouts, blogs and e-mails, finding aids and web pages. The goal is the same, to use your knowledge of boys and literature to connect boys with the books that speak to them. In some ways it is easier than face-to-face readers' advisory; you can take time, edit your words, add visuals, and generally make everything work nicely. In one important way, indirect readers' advisory has a major challenge. You do not have information about your audience. You are working blind, so you must apply all your knowledge to tailor your audience as well as tailoring your message. Placement is important; you must promote the right books in the right place and the right way to reach the audience you are most likely to encounter. Volume is another way to counteract this lack of communication; you need to promote many books in many ways and many venues. This is where readers' advisory meets public relations.

Why do indirect readers' advisory? Because you will not always be there when a boy needs you. Indirect readers' advisory extends your service hours. Maybe there will not be anyone there to help when a boy needs a book, and maybe the person who is there will not be as knowledgeable and committed to helping boys read as you are. Maybe a boy will need to pick a book when your school or library is closed, late at night or on a holiday. If it is true that many boys are reluctant readers, you cannot miss an opportunity to bring them to books. There are ways to take your skills and knowledge and apply them beyond the walls of your building or the borders of your town.

Most important, indirect readers' advisory has the potential to reach those boys who would not usually ask you for help. Maybe they harbor negative perceptions about libraries, or education in general, so they will not come into your library and ask you for a book. Maybe they are uncomfortable about sharing their tastes or abilities with adults, so they will come into your library but will not ask you for a book. Maybe they just find working in the electronic world more comfortable. All of these are perfectly reasonable restrictions, at least from the boy's point of view, and anything we can do to serve these boys we should do.

Indirect readers' advisory leverages the work you do every day, so it is essential that you find ways to capture the readers' advisory you do in person. You can log your personal reading, the books you suggest to boys during your work, and their reaction to those books. Readers' advisory is best as an ongoing conversation, so always invite readers to tell you what they think of the books you suggest, and on those occasions when they do, make sure you capture that. You can log the suggestions you hear from others, and log the sources you use when you perform readers' advisory. Mostly, you must find ways to allow readers to suggest books to other readers. In this way, your job as a readers' advisor becomes that of a guide. Although indirect readers' advisory may seem like a lot of work, the information is already there. You simply have to package what you already have, and what others can provide, for new and varied formats.

WRITE IT DOWN!

Librarians for years have used the print medium to promote reading. Bibliographies and other less-formal finding aids are familiar enough. The downside of these mediums is that they often appeal to an already active reading audience. Although there are certainly active boy readers, it is dangerous to limit your outreach to these. There are already many established aids for such readers. Much like readers' advisory in person, indirect readers' advisory should always be done with an eye toward promoting reading itself, as well as promoting particular titles, to those readers who need the most help.

How do you reach out to a nonreading audience using a traditional written format? Boys who do not read may well be wary of a bibliography, associating it with academics, seeing it as bookish, and maybe remembering getting very dull books off of a bibliography in the past. Collect the bibliographies that are most likely to fall into the hands of the boys you are trying to reach, and do your best to differentiate your list from those. That should get you on the right path.

Bibliographies often approach subjects, but with little variance in form, format, or genre. When trying to reach boys, it is often effective to list print and nonprint materials, real world and virtual sites, fiction and nonfiction, and books across the genres. Remember that many boys think of reading as a means to an end, that end usually being understanding of something in their lives. It is the content of reading, not the process, that appeals to many boys. We often think of reading as an end in itself and create bibliographies in that way. Many boys are more interested in the what, not the how.

The information we provide can also affect how boys see our bibliographies. When we add information that does not help a boy either choose or find a book, such as publisher, city of publication, ISBN, or LCCN, we make the bibliography look academic. Although we may wish readers would be interested in such information, the fact of the matter is that this information has nothing really to do with choosing a book.

On the other hand, we often do not include the information readers really need. It is a truism that annotated bibliographies are more useful than nonannotated bibliographies, and this is especially true for reluctant or resistant readers and those with less background and experience. Just listing a book by a famous author may be enough to catch the eye of a child who has read extensively, but those who have not will need more. What we add to an annotation is important as well. Although an exhaustive review may appeal to our sense of professional duty, we need to consider the effect on different readers. Avid readers may well see the good and bad in a review and be willing to make an educated decision about what to read, but a child who reads less and has less trust in an adult's recommendations often reads these reviews with an eye toward elimination. He is looking for reasons not to read the book, and he may ignore all the reasons you list to read it. Annotations for boys should be closer to your booktalks than book reviews.

What you do with your bibliographies matters as well. Printing out a full-page finding aid, in good bibliographic order and consisting entirely of formal text, and then leaving it on a library desk or literature rack may not be the most appealing, not for anyone and especially not for boys. Think first about what you want your bibliography to say about reading and about the books on the list; then ask yourself how the formatting of the list can send that message. Illustrated books often have great boy appeal; do you need to add visual elements to your bibliography? The collectible-card format has shown amazing staying power, moving from the sports card to hero cards to role-playing game cards. Police departments are producing hero cards for their officers to introduce themselves to youth. Why not adopt this format for books? Produce cards (two-sided printing on heavy-stock paper) with cover art on the front and a booktalk and your library info on the back. If you get these into the right hands, you can practically sit back and watch the boys come in for the books.

Where do you need to put such cards and bibliographies for them to have the greatest effect? Are you trying to reach boys who do not use your library? Then placing such items in your library is obviously not the right approach. Think of where boys gather and why. A sports venue is a great place to put a finding aid for sports books. A leaders' meeting of the Boy Scouts is a great place to put an annotated list of outdoor adventure books, turning Scout leaders into instruments of your readers' advisory. If there is concern that boys are spending all their time online and not enough time with books, then online sites (not just your library's) are the way to go. Consider an extremely short bibliography, maybe a bibliography of a single title, with cover art and a booktalk, maybe even testimonials of real local kids, in the form of a poster that you can reproduce and spread around. A list of one does not a bibliography make, you say? If it gets a boy to read, do not quibble over definitions.

Inside your library, the list approach loses a great deal of its appeal. Why tell a potential reader that books exist somewhere, even if that some-where is only a few feet away, when you could simply put the book in his hands? We do not use displays to their great advantage in most libraries. If you think you use displays effectively, double their use in your library, and you may be shocked by your success. If you do not feel you use displays effectively, then you have all the more work to do. The principle is simple: strike while the iron is hot. If you can get the attention of a boy with a description of a book, do not risk him not finding the book before his interest wanes. Get him interested in the book itself; then hand him the book.

Librarians are hesitant to use displays because they take books out of shelf-list order, and they lean on bibliographies because these instruments promote books even if the books are currently checked out. Both approaches ignore some realities that apply to all library users to some degree but to boys especially. First, our nice, neat shelf order is of little appeal to casual users, who might be better served by using a bookstore-style subject organization to begin with. Our desire to find a book in its exact location translates to the casual user as needing to find one exact location in order to find a book. Librarians for generations have laughed about users who ask us why we do not simply put a box out front marked "The Good Books." It is time to stop laughing and adopt this suggestion.

I would frequently put a shelving cart in the middle of the children's room with a sign that read "Books for Guys," then restock it a few times per day as the books disappeared. The sign was the shortest, and most effective, booktalk I ever gave, and because it was in the form of indirect readers' advisory, it reached kids whether I was in the library or not. A hint for this or any other display aimed at popular interest: always leave space for an "I Recommend" section that encourages boys to place their own favorites on the shelf. It reaffirms boys as readers, allows boys to receive recommendations from peers, and builds up communities of readers.

As for promoting books that are checked out, it is of limited use to tell a boy that there is a great book for him to read—and we can get it for him when it is returned, in two weeks. So much of boys' reading is outwardly directed: get a book now, says the teacher or the mom. In two weeks, he hopes, he will no longer need to get a book. Even if the reading is self-directed, the interest tends to be immediate. There are few boys who carry around little notebooks where they jot down books they want to read someday. The worst-case scenario may be the boy who believes you, that this is the perfect book for him to read, and simply waits two weeks for the book instead of reading something that you told him was inferior. No, it is best to put books in his hands, not in his head.

READERS' ADVISORY ONLINE

The online world is an ideal place to do indirect readers' advisory. It is a place where many boys spend a great deal of time, especially those boys you see little of in the library. A 2005 Kaiser Family Foundation survey found that the average U.S. child spends 6.5 hours per day watching TV, using computers, or engaging in other electronic activities.[1] A good deal of that time is clearly spent online, and if 6.5 hours a day is the average, that means many kids are spending even more time in front of an electronic screen. And the more time they spend online, the less time they spend in front of you. Go find those kids. Every bit of readers' advisory you put on paper needs to be put online somehow, and as much as possible, it needs to be interactive.

Online readers' advisory can be as simple as creating a page on your library's website where you post your booktalks as you write them. Making it interactive can be as simple as adding an e-mail link that asks readers to comment on your booktalks or send in their own. Collect the e-mails, cut and paste the text onto your page, and you have interaction, albeit on a pretty simple level. Now start adding appeal.

Capture your booktalks on audio and podcast them. A podcast is, simply put, an audio clip that you make available online. All you need is a computer, a microphone, and some easily accessible software. The hows and whys are available in a book by Nancy J. Keane and Terence W. Cavanaugh titled *The Tech-Savvy Booktalker: A Guide for 21st-Century Educators* (Libraries Unlimited, 2009). Keane has long led the way in pod-casting booktalks for kids on her website: "Booktalks—Quick and Simple" (www.nancykeane.com/booktalks/). You can use her site and others like it for examples of how to do a podcast but also to build a collection of links to make available to your kids. Why then do your own? Because you have a relationship with your kids, and that has a different kind of appeal. Also, others may want to add your content to their resources. Remember, indirect readers' advisory leverages your work by making it available at different times and in different places, and with the Web, the reach is unlimited.

Once you begin recording your booktalks for podcast, the next natural step is to get your kids to do the same. Again, Keane and Cavanaugh's book will give you all the direction you could need. Why have boys record their own booktalks? Simply put, some boys will be far more comfortable talking in front of a microphone than in front of a human audience. There are fewer issues of embarrassment, and frankly, the technological aspects have special appeal to many tool-inspired boys. Of course, whatever is said about audio is twice as effective with video. There is more specialized equipment involved, and a bit more complexity, but video has more impact all around than audio. Posting video clips of kids doing booktalks is simple enough using YouTube (www.youtube.com), and once the clips are posted, kids will do much of the promotional work for you, telling all their friends, both real and virtual, to "check it out."

YouTube is just one of the many tools available for use online. Blog sites such as eBlogger (www.eblogger.com) and Blogger (www.blogger .com), Google's blog utility, let you create an outreach tool through which you can simply post booktalks that you write as you write them. Every day you can simply list the books that kids tell you they love and why. Not only does a blog allow you to actually do readers' advisory but it tells kids, parents, teachers, and other librarians that you are someone they can come to for readers' advisory. For boys this can be especially effective, as online readers' advisory is interactive but at arm's length. Most blog sites make it easy to post audio and video as well.

Social networking sites are probably the most effective vehicle for online readers' advisory available today. Social networking sites create an ongoing connection between online users that can be used for both quick and ephemeral updates and static posting of materials like pictures, multimedia clips, and text. All of these traits are useful enough for doing readers' advisory. Sites such as Facebook (www.facebook.com), and My-Space (www.myspace.com) are almost ubiquitous today, and your kids are certainly on them. These sites are also a great venue to post or refer to videos available on YouTube. Be willing to adjust, though; these sites rose out of nowhere, and the next big site will appear before you finish reading this chapter.

One social networking site that you can promote specifically to reach young readers is Goodreads (www.goodreads.com). This site is primarily a running online reading log for users that is accessible to the "friends" with whom they connect online. In addition to listing books to read, books currently being read, and books read, users can rate books, review them, and recommend them to others. You can join, list your books, and post your booktalks as reviews; then encourage your kids to join as well. When they "friend" you, they can see your reading and share theirs with you and all their friends. Indeed, that sharing is automatic, with daily updates coming whenever any one of your friends posts a review or updates his or her book lists. There are online discussion groups as well, ideal for the genre-infatuated reader. One great feature of Goodreads is the number of authors who have joined and set up author pages. Your kids can search for their favorite authors and connect with them online to comment on their reading and ask questions.

CONCLUSION

Although the art of readers' advisory is in the personal interaction involved, the science is in the indirect approach. If every bit of your knowledge and experience is captured in some way and accessible in a number of formats, you double and triple the impact of what you do. Librarians may value the personal approach, with the ability to do a quality readers' advisory interview, the chance to show your passion, and the experience of seeing the young readers' reactions. But if the goal is to reach kids, it must be their needs and perspectives that shape what we do. That perspective will be varied, and varied approaches must be used to reach kids how, where, and when they are receptive.

Boys especially may need to be approached differently because so many of them sense a gap, real or imaginary, between the library and their everyday lives. Spanning that gap does not necessarily mean a great deal of extra work for the librarian. The raw materials of readers' advisory are already there in the work you do every day and in the peer-to-peer readers' advisory you can facilitate. Capture and reuse all the readers' advisory you do, and make it available in new ways and places, and you will create a world of books through which your boys can travel on whatever path they choose.

NOTE

1. Marilyn Elias, "Electronic World Swallows Up Kids' Time, Study Finds," *USA Today* (March 10, 2005): A1.

CHAPTER 10

BOOK LISTS FOR BOYS
Nonfiction

Nonfiction, of course, covers such a huge range of subjects and formats that any attempt to list recommended books seems to be an impossible undertaking. There are great books on everything from nature to sports to crime and adventure. This is a list of just some of the titles that stand out. Many of these authors have a huge list of titles worth checking out as well. The age suggestions are general at best, meant to be helpful, not restrictive. They portray the books' intended audience but not necessarily reading level or any judgment of appropriateness.

NONFICTION BOOKS FOR ELEMENTARY SCHOOL BOYS

Karen Chin and Thom Holmes. *Dino Dung: The Scoop on Fossil Feces.* Random House, 2004.

Susan E. Goodman. Illustrated by Elwood H. Smith. *Gee Whiz! It's All about Pee.* Viking, 2006.

———. Illustrated by Elwood H. Smith. *The Truth about Poop.* Viking, 2004.

Kathleen Kudlinski. *Boy, Were We Wrong about Dinosaurs!* Dutton, 2005.

Marilyn Singer. *What Stinks?* Darby Creek, 2006.

Desiree Webber. *Bonehead: Story of the Longhorn.* Eakin, 2003.

———. *The Buffalo Train Ride.* Eakin, 1999.

NONFICTION BOOKS FOR MIDDLE SCHOOL BOYS

John Fleischman. *Phineas Gage: A Gruesome but True Story about Brain Science.* Houghton Mifflin, 2002.

Paul Fleisher. *Parasites: Latching On to a Free Lunch.* Twenty-First Century Books, 2006.

Thomas R. Holtz and Luis V. Rey. *Dinosaurs: The Most Complete, Up-to-Date Encyclopedia for Dinosaur Lovers of All Ages.* Random House, 2007.

Sandra Markle. *Outside and Inside Mummies.* Walker, 2005.

Kadir Nelson. *We Are the Ship: The Story of Negro League Baseball.* Jump at the Sun, 2008.

Nathaniel Philbrick. *Revenge of the Whale: The True Story of the Whaleship Essex.* Putnam, 2002.

Andrew Solway. *What's Living in Your Bedroom?* Heinemann, 2004.

NONFICTION BOOKS FOR HIGH SCHOOL BOYS

Bill Bryson. *A Walk in the Woods: Rediscovering America on the Appalachian Trail.* Broadway, 1998.

Jack Gantos. *Hole in My Life.* Farrar, Straus, and Giroux, 2002.

David Grann. *The Lost City of Z: A Tale of Deadly Obsession in the Amazon.* Doubleday, 2009.

William Gurstelle. *The Art of the Catapult: Build Greek Ballistae, Roman Onagers, English Trebuchets, and More Ancient Artillery.* Chicago Review, 2004.

————. *Backyard Ballistics.* Chicago Review, 2001.

Jon Krakauer. *Into Thin Air: A Personal Account of the Mount Everest Disaster.* Villard, 1997.

Roland Laird and Taneshia Nash Laird. *Still I Rise: A Graphic History of African Americans.* Sterling, 2009.

Michael Lewis. *The Blind Side: Evolution of a Game.* Norton, 2007.

Deborah Noyes. *Encyclopedia of the End: Mysterious Death in Fact, Fancy, Folklore, and More.* Houghton Mifflin, 2008.

Cal Ripken Jr. and Mike Bryan. *The Only Way I Know.* Viking, 1997.

Ken Silverstein. *The Radioactive Boy Scout: The True Story of a Boy and His Backyard Nuclear Reactor.* Random House, 2004.

James L. Swanson. *Chasing Lincoln's Killer.* Scholastic, 2009.

Stanley "Tookie" Williams. *Life in Prison.* Chronicle, 2001.

TRIVIA, MINUTIAE, LISTS, AND ENCYCLOPEDIC FUN

Boys love trivia. It is short, interesting, often edgy, and it sheds light on the world they love to explore. Promoting these books is easy, too. You stand up and read a few passages, and let them take it from there. Being encyclopedic, most of these appeal to a broad range of ages, so they are listed here together.

Sylvia Branzei. *Animal Grossology.* Price Stern Sloan, 2004.

———. *Grossology.* Price Stern Sloan, 2002.

———. *Grossology and You.* Price Stern Sloan, 2002.

———. *Hands-On Grossology.* Price Stern Sloan, 2003.

James Buckley. *The Bathroom Companion: A Collection of Facts about the Most-Used Room in the House.* Quirk, 2005.

Samantha Ettus. *The Experts' Guide to 100 Things Everyone Should Know.* Clarkson Potter, 2004.

Joy Masoff. *Oh Yikes! History's Grossest, Wackiest Moments.* Workman, 2006.

———. *Oh Yuck! The Encyclopedia of Everything Nasty.* Workman, 2000.

Jennifer Morse. *Guinness Book of World Records, 2009.* Scholastic, 2008.

Joshua Piven and David Borgenicht. *The Worst-Case Scenario Survival Handbook.* Chronicle, 1999.

———. *The Worst-Case Scenario Survival Handbook: Extreme Edition.* Chronicle, 2005.

Nancy Rica Schiff. *Odd Jobs: Portraits of Unusual Occupations.* Ten Speed, 2002.

———. *Odder Jobs: More Portraits of Unusual Occupations.* Ten Speed, 2006.

Ripley's Believe It or Not Special Edition, 2009. Scholastic, 2008.

James Solheim. *It's Disgusting and We Ate It! True Food Facts from Around the World and Throughout History.* Simon and Schuster, 1998.

Stephen Spignesi. *The Weird 100: A Collection of the Strange and the Unexplained.* Citadel, 2004.

This Book Really Sucks! The Science behind Gravity, Flight, Leeches, Black Holes, Tornadoes, Our Friend the Vacuum Cleaner, and Most Everything Else That Sucks. Planet Dexter, 1999.

Chris Woodford. *Cool Stuff Exploded*. Dorling Kindersley, 2008.

——. *How Cool Stuff Works*. Dorling Kindersley, 2008.

Chris Woodford and Jon Woodcock. *Cool Stuff 2.0 and How It Works*. Dorling Kindersley, 2007.

——. *The Gadget Book: How Really Cool Stuff Works*. Dorling Kindersley, 2007.

Chris Woodford et al. *Cool Stuff and How It Works*. Dorling Kindersley, 2005.

CHAPTER 11

BOOK LISTS FOR BOYS
Humor

Humor creates its own problems when it comes to assigning age categories. The humor that appeals to boys tends to be edgy, making a book look older than its intended audience. At the same time, it is designed for high appeal even to reluctant readers, so the reading level may be aimed well below the intended audience. The age suggestions here are general at best. Do your best to see these books for what they are, a chance for fun, laughter, and some guilty pleasure. Stressing out over age appropriateness defeats the purpose.

HUMOR FOR ELEMENTARY SCHOOL BOYS

Kevin Bolger. *Sir Fartsalot Hunts the Booger.* Penguin, 2008.

Eoin Colfer. Eoin Colfer's Legend Of . . . series.

    Legend of Spud Murphy. Miramax, 2004.

    Legend of Captain Crow's Teeth. Miramax, 2005.

    Legend of the Worst Boy in the World. Hyperion, 2008.

D. L. Garfinkle. Supernatural Rubber Chicken series.

    Fowl Language. Mirrorstone, 2008.

    Fine Feathered Four Eyes. Mirrorstone, 2008.

    Poultry in Motion. Mirrorstone, 2008.

Dan Gutman. *The Get Rich Quick Club.* HarperCollins, 2004.

Jeff Kinney. Diary of a Wimpy Kid series.

    Diary of a Wimpy Kid. Amulet, 2007.

Diary of a Wimpy Kid: Rodrick Rules. Amulet, 2008.

Diary of a Wimpy Kid: The Last Straw. Amulet, 2009.

Erik P. Kraft. Lenny and Mel series.

Lenny and Mel. Simon and Schuster, 2002.

Lenny and Mel's Summer Vacation. Simon and Schuster, 2003.

Lenny and Mel: After-School Confidential. Simon and Schuster, 2004.

David Lubar. *Punished!* Darby Creek, 2006.

Laurie Myers. *Surviving Brick Johnson.* Clarion, 2000.

Ken Roberts. *The Thumb in the Box.* Douglas and McIntyre, 2001.

———. *Thumb on a Diamond.* Groundwood, 2006.

———. *Thumb and the Bad Guys.* Groundwood, 2009.

Louis Sachar. Wayside School series.

Sideways Stories from Wayside School. HarperCollins, 1978.

Wayside School Is Falling Down. HarperCollins, 1989.

Sideways Arithmetic from Wayside School. HarperCollins, 1989.

More Sideways Arithmetic from Wayside School. HarperCollins, 1994.

Wayside School Gets a Little Stranger. HarperCollins, 1995.

Pam Smallcomb. *The Last Burp of Mac McGerp.* Bloomsbury, 2004.

Michael Sullivan. Escapade Johnson series.

Escapade Johnson and Mayhem at Mount Moosilauke. PublishingWorks, 2006.

Escapade Johnson and the Coffee Shop of the Living Dead. PublishingWorks, 2008.

Escapade Johnson and the Witches of Belknap County. PublishingWorks, 2008.

Escapade Johnson and the Phantom of the Science Fair. PublishingWorks, 2009.

Henry Winkler and Lin Oliver. Hank Zipzer series.

Niagara Falls, or Does It? Grosset and Dunlap, 2003.

I Got a D in Salami. Grosset and Dunlap, 2003.

Day of the Iguana. Grosset and Dunlap, 2003.

Zippity Zinger. Grosset and Dunlap, 2003.

The Night I Flunked My Field Trip. Grosset and Dunlap, 2004.

Holy Enchilada! Grosset and Dunlap, 2004.

Help! Somebody Get Me Out of Fourth Grade. Grosset and Dunlap, 2004.

Summer School! What Genius Thought That Up? Grosset and Dunlap, 2005.

The Secret Life of a Ping-Pong Wizard. Grosset and Dunlap, 2005.

My Dog's a Scaredy-Cat. Grosset and Dunlap, 2006.

The Curtain Went Up, My Pants Fell Down. Grosset and Dunlap, 2007.

Barfing in the Backseat: How I Survived My Family Road Trip. Grosset and Dunlap, 2007.

Who Ordered This Baby? Definitely Not Me! Grosset and Dunlap, 2007.

The Life of Me: Enter at Your Own Risk. Grosset and Dunlap, 2008.

A Tale of Two Tails. Grosset and Dunlap, 2008.

HUMOR FOR MIDDLE SCHOOL BOYS

Gennifer Choldenko. *Al Capone Does My Shirts.* Putnam, 2004.

Jack Gantos. Joey Pigza series.

Joey Pigza Swallowed the Key. Farrar, Strauss, and Giroux, 1998.

Joey Pigza Loses Control. Farrar, Strauss, and Giroux, 2000.

What Would Joey Do? Farrar, Strauss, and Giroux, 2002.

Morris Gleitzman. *Toad Rage.* Random House, 2004.

———. *Toad Heaven.* Random House, 2005.

———. *Toad Away.* Random House, 2006.

Andy Griffiths. *The Day My Butt Went Psycho.* Scholastic, 2003.

———. *Zombie Butts from Uranus.* Scholastic, 2004.

———. *Butt Wars! The Final Conflict.* Scholastic, 2005.

Gordon Korman. *Schooled.* Hyperion, 2007.

———. *The 6th Grade Nickname Game.* Hyperion, 2007.

Blake Nelson. *Gender Blender.* Delacorte, 2006.

Gary Paulsen. *Harris and Me.* Harcourt, 1993.

Richard Peck. *The Teacher's Funeral: A Comedy in Three Acts.* Dial, 2004.

Jerry Spinelli. *Loser.* Joanna Cotler, 2002.

Todd Strasser. Help! I'm Trapped . . . series.

Help! I'm Trapped in My Teacher's Body. Scholastic, 1993.

Help! I'm Trapped in the First Day of School. Scholastic, 1994.

Help! I'm Trapped in Obedience School. Scholastic, 1995.

Help! I'm Trapped in My Gym Teacher's Body. Scholastic, 1996.

Help! I'm Trapped in the President's Body. Scholastic, 1997.

Help! I'm Trapped in Obedience School Again. Scholastic, 1997.

Help! I'm Trapped in My Sister's Body. Scholastic, 1997.

Help! I'm Trapped in the First Day of Summer Camp. Scholastic, 1997.

Help! I'm Trapped in Santa's Body. Scholastic, 1997.

Help! I'm Trapped in My Principal's Body. Scholastic, 1998.

Help! I'm Trapped in an Alien's Body. Apple, 1998.

Help! I'm Trapped in My Camp Counselor's Body. Apple, 1998.

Help! I'm Trapped in a Movie Star's Body. Apple, 1999.

Help! I'm Trapped in My Lunch Lady's Body. Scholastic, 1999.

Help! I'm Trapped in a Vampire's Body. Scholastic, 2000.

Help! I'm Trapped in a Professional Wrestler's Body. Scholastic, 2000.

Help! I'm Trapped in a Supermodel's Body. Apple, 2001.

Help! I'm Trapped in Summer Camp. Scholastic, 2006.

Todd Strasser. *Is That a Sick Cat in Your Backpack?* Scholastic, 2007.

———. *Is That a Dead Dog in Your Locker?* Scholastic, 2008.

———. *Is That a Glow-in-the-Dark Bunny in Your Pillowcase?* Scholastic 2009.

Wendelin Van Draanen. *Swear to Howdy.* Knopf, 2003.

HUMOR FOR HIGH SCHOOL BOYS

Terence Blacker. *Boy 2 Girl.* Farrar, Straus, and Giroux, 2005.

———. *Parent Swap.* Farrar, Straus, and Giroux, 2006.

D. L. Garfinkle. *Storky: How I Lost My Nickname and Won the Girl.* Putnam, 2005.

Carl Hiaasen. *Flush.* Knopf, 2005.

———. *Hoot.* Knopf, 2002.

———. *Scat.* Knopf, 2009.

Gordon Korman. *Born to Rock.* Hyperion, 2006.

———. *No More Dead Dogs.* Hyperion, 2002.

———. *Son of the Mob.* Hyperion, 2002.

———. *Son of the Mob: Hollywood Hustle.* Hyperion, 2004.

Christopher Moore. *Fluke; or, I Know Why the Winged Whale Sings.* Morrow, 2003.

———. *Lamb: The Gospel According to Biff, Christ's Childhood Pal.* Morrow, 2002.

CHAPTER 12

BOOK LISTS FOR BOYS
Fantasy

Fantasy is the broadest and most varied of the boy genres. Indeed, there are subgenres that are aimed particularly at girls, but there are many more that have real boy appeal. What holds these subgenres together and makes them all part of the fantasy family is their focus on a world that is not. It might be a world that may have been, that might be now if things had gone differently, that might be now in a different dimension or in a hollow under a stone in your own backyard. Fantasy stories work not by the rules of science and logic but by rules set by the author. Once again, the age breakdowns are meant to give the most general of guidance. Think about how hard it would be to place the Harry Potter books in a single age category! Fantasy readers are famous for reading well above their apparent reading level because of intense interest. Be willing to let those boys go as far as they are willing to go. Look to the end of the chapter for suggestions from the emerging subgenres of humor fantasy, magic-free fantasy, and martial arts fantasy.

FANTASY FOR ELEMENTARY SCHOOL BOYS

Tony Abbott. The Secrets of Droon series.

The Hidden Stairs and the Magic Carpet. Scholastic, 1999.

Journey to the Volcano Palace. Scholastic, 1999.

The Mysterious Island. Scholastic, 1999.

City in the Clouds. Scholastic, 1999.

The Great Ice Battle. Scholastic, 1999.

The Sleeping Giant of Goll. Scholastic, 2000.

Into the Land of the Lost. Scholastic, 2000.

The Golden Wasp. Scholastic, 2000.

Tower of the Elf King. Scholastic, 2000.

Quest for the Queen. Scholastic, 2000.

The Hawk Bandits of Tarkoom. Scholastic, 2001.

Under the Serpent Sea. Scholastic, 2001.

The Mask of Maliban. Scholastic, 2001.

Voyage of the Jaffa Wind. Scholastic, 2002.

The Moon Scroll. Scholastic, 2002.

The Knights of Silversnow. Scholastic, 2002.

The Dream Thief. Scholastic, 2003.

Search for the Dragon Ship. Scholastic, 2003.

The Coiled Viper. Scholastic, 2003.

The Ice Caves of Krog. Scholastic, 2003.

Flight of the Genie. Scholastic, 2004.

The Isle of Mists. Scholastic, 2004.

The Fortress of the Treasure Queen. Scholastic, 2004.

The Race to Doobesh. Scholastic, 2005.

The Riddle of Zorfendorf Castle. Scholastic, 2005.

The Moon Dragon. Scholastic, 2006.

In the Shadow of Goll. Scholastic, 2006.

Pirates of the Purple Dawn. Scholastic, 2007.

Escape from Jabar-Loo. Scholastic, 2007.

Queen of Shadowthorn. Scholastic, 2007.

Moon Magic. Scholastic, 2008.

The Treasure of the Orkins. Scholastic, 2008.

Flight of the Blue Serpent. Scholastic, 2008.

In the City of Dreams. Scholastic, 2009.

Crown of Wizards. Scholastic, 2009.

Ridley Pearson and Dave Barry. Never Land series.

Escape from the Carnivale. Disney, 2006.

Cave of the Dark Wind. Disney, 2007.

Blood Tide. Disney, 2008.

Jon Scieszka. The Time Warp Trio series.

Knights of the Kitchen Table. Viking, 1991.

The Not-So-Jolly Roger. Viking, 1991.

The Good, the Bad, and the Goofy. Viking, 1992.

Your Mother Was a Neanderthal. Viking, 1993.

2095. Viking, 1995.

Tut Tut. Viking, 1996.

Summer Reading Is Killing Me. Viking, 1998.

It's All Greek to Me. Viking, 1999.

See You Later, Gladiator. Viking, 2000.

Sam Samurai. Viking, 2001.

Hey Kid, Want to Buy a Bridge? Viking, 2002.

Viking It and Liking It. Viking, 2002.

Me Oh Maya. Viking, 2003.

Da Wild, Da Crazy, Da Vinci. Viking, 2004.

Oh Say, I Can't See. Viking, 2005.

Marco? Polo! Viking, 2006.

Nightmare on Joe's Street. Viking, 2006.

Lewis and Clark . . . and Jodi, Freddi, and Samantha. Viking, 2006.

The Seven Blunders of the World. Viking, 2006.

Vivian Vande Velde. *Wizard at Work.* Magic Carpet Books, 2003.

FANTASY FOR MIDDLE SCHOOL BOYS

Dave Barry and Ridley Pearson. The Starcatchers series.

Peter and the Starcatchers. Disney, 2004.

Peter and the Shadow Thieves. Disney, 2006.

Peter and the Secret of Rundoon. Disney, 2007.

Royce Buckingham. *Demonkeeper.* Putnam, 2007.

———. *Goblins! An UnderEarth Adventure.* Putnam, 2008.

Ann Downer. *Hatching Magic.* Aladdin, 2003.

Emily Drake. The Magickers series.

The Magickers. DAW, 2001.

The Curse of Arkady. DAW, 2002.

The Dragon Guard. DAW, 2003.

The Gate of Bones. DAW, 2004.

Jeanne DuPrau. Books of Ember series.

The City of Ember. Random House, 2003.

The People of Sparks. Random House, 2004.

The Prophet of Yonwood. Random House, 2006.

The Diamond of Darkhold. Random House, 2008.

Nancy Farmer. *Sea of Trolls.* Atheneum, 2004.

John Flanagan. Ranger's Apprentice series.

The Ruins of Gorlan. Puffin, 2005.

The Burning Bridge. Philomel, 2006.

The Icebound Land. Philomel, 2007.

The Battle for Skandia. Philomel, 2008.

The Sorcerer of the North. Philomel, 2008.

The Siege of Macindaw. Philomel, 2009.

Julie Hahnke. The Wolf's Apprentice series.

The Grey Ghost. PublishingWorks, 2009.

Kate Klimo and John Shroades. Dragon Keepers series.

The Dragon in the Sock Drawer. Random House, 2008.

The Dragon in the Driveway. Random House, 2009.

D. J. MacHale. Pendragon series.

The Merchant of Death. Aladdin, 2002.

The Lost City of Faar. Aladdin, 2003.

The Never War. Aladdin, 2003.

The Reality Bug. Aladdin, 2003.

Black Water. Aladdin, 2004.

The Rivers of Zadaa. Simon and Schuster, 2005.

The Quillan Games. Simon and Schuster, 2006.

The Pilgrims of Rayne. Simon and Schuster, 2007.

Raven Rise. Simon and Schuster, 2008.

The Soldiers of Halla. Aladdin, 2009.

Kenneth Oppel. *Silverwing.* Simon and Schuster, 1997.

———. *Sunwing.* Simon and Schuster, 2000.

———. *Firewing.* Simon and Schuster, 2003.

————. *Darkwing*. Simon and Schuster, 2007.

Rick Riordan. Percy Jackson and the Olympians series.

The Lightning Thief. Miramax, 2005.

The Sea of Monsters. Miramax, 2006.

The Titan's Curse. Miramax, 2007.

The Battle of the Labyrinth. Hyperion, 2008.

The Demigod Files. Hyperion, 2009.

The Last Olympian. Hyperion, 2009.

Emily Rodda. Deltora Quest series.

The Forests of Silence. Apple, 2001.

The Lake of Tears. Apple, 2001.

City of the Rats. Apple, 2001.

The Shifting Sands. Apple, 2001.

Dread Mountain. Apple, 2001.

The Maze of the Beast. Apple, 2001.

The Valley of the Lost. Apple, 2001.

Return to Del. Scholastic, 2001.

Tales of Deltora. Scholastic, 2006.

Emily Rodda. Deltora Shadowlands series.

Cavern of Fear. Scholastic, 2002.

Isle of Illusion. Scholastic, 2002.

The Shadowlands. Scholastic, 2002.

The Book of Monsters. Scholastic, 2002.

Emily Rodda. Dragons of Deltora series.

Dragon's Nest. Scholastic, 2004.

Shadowgate. Scholastic, 2004.

Isle of the Dead. Scholastic, 2004.

Sister of the South. Scholastic, 2005.

J. K. Rowling. Harry Potter series.

Harry Potter and the Sorcerer's Stone. Scholastic, 1998.

Harry Potter and the Chamber of Secrets. Scholastic, 1999.

Harry Potter and the Prisoner of Azkaban. Scholastic, 1999.

Harry Potter and the Goblet of Fire. Scholastic, 2000.

Harry Potter and the Order of the Phoenix. Arthur A. Levine Books, 2003.

Harry Potter and the Half-Blood Prince. Scholastic, 2005.

Harry Potter and the Deathly Hallows. Scholastic, 2007.

Louis Sachar. *Holes.* Farrar, Straus, and Giroux, 1998.

Jeff Stone. The Five Ancestors series.

Tiger. Random House, 2005.

Monkey. Random House, 2005.

Snake. Random House, 2006.

Crane. Random House, 2007.

Eagle. Random House, 2008.

Mouse. Random House, 2009.

Jonathan Stroud. *Heroes of the Valley.* Hyperion, 2009.

Michael Sullivan. The Bard series.

The Sapphire Knight. PublishingWorks, 2009.

J. R. R. Tolkien. *The Hobbit.* Graphia, 2002.

David Ward. The Grassland Trilogy series.

Escape the Mask. Amulet, 2008.

Beneath the Mask. Amulet, 2008.

FANTASY FOR HIGH SCHOOL BOYS

Philip Caveney. Sebastian Darke series.

Sebastian Darke, Prince of Fools. Delacorte, 2008.

Sebastian Darke, Prince of Pirates. Delacorte, 2009.

Kathleen Duey. A Resurrection of Magic series.

Skin Hunger. Atheneum, 2007.

Sacred Scars. Atheneum, 2009.

David Eddings. The Elenium series.

The Diamond Throne. Del Rey, 1989.

The Ruby Knight. Del Rey, 1990.

The Sapphire Rose. Del Rey, 1991.

David Eddings. The Tamuli series.

Domes of Fire. Del Rey, 1993.

The Shining Ones. Del Rey, 1993.

Hidden City. Del Rey, 1994.

David Elliott. *Jeremy Cabbage and the Living Museum of Human Oddballs and Quadruped Delights.* Knopf, 2008.

Nancy Farmer. *The House of the Scorpion.* Atheneum, 2002.

Alison Goodman. *Eon: Dragoneye Reborn.* Viking, 2008.

Lian Hearn. Tales of the Otori series.

> *Heaven's Net Is Wide.* Riverhead, 2007. [Prequel]
>
> *The Sword of the Warrior: Across the Nightingale Floor, Episode 1.* Puffin, 2004.
>
> *Journey to Inuyama: Across the Nightingale Floor, Episode 2.* Puffin, 2005.
>
> *Lord Fujiwara's Treasures: Grass for His Pillow, Episode 1.* Puffin, 2005.
>
> *The Way through the Snow: Grass for His Pillow, Episode 2.* Puffin, 2005.
>
> *Battle for Maruyama: Brilliance of the Moon, Episode 1.* Puffin, 2006.
>
> *Scars of Victory: Brilliance of the Moon, Episode 2.* Puffin, 2006.
>
> *The Harsh Cry of the Heron: The Last Tale of the Otori.* Riverhead, 2007.

Chris Humphreys. The Runestone Saga series.

> *The Fetch.* Knopf, 2006.
>
> *Vendetta.* Knopf, 2007.
>
> *Possession.* Knopf, 2008.

Christopher Moore. *Fluke; or, I Know Why the Winged Whale Sings.* Morrow, 2003.

P. R. Moredun. *The Dragon Conspiracy.* HarperCollins, 2005.

Christopher Paolini. Inheritance series.

> *Eragon.* Knopf, 2003.
>
> *Eldest.* Knopf, 2005.
>
> *Brisingr.* Knopf, 2008.

Terry Pratchett. Discworld series. [Plot Order]

> *The Color of Magic.* HarperTorch, 2000.
>
> *The Light Fantastic.* HarperTorch, 2000.
>
> *Equal Rites.* HarperTorch, 2005.
>
> *Mort.* HarperTorch, 2001.
>
> *Sourcery.* HarperTorch, 2001.
>
> *Wyrd Sisters.* HarperTorch, 2001.
>
> *Pyramids.* HarperTorch, 2001.
>
> *Guards! Guards!* HarperTorch, 2001.
>
> *Eric.* HarperTorch, 2002.

Moving Pictures. HarperTorch, 2002.

Reaper Man. HarperTorch, 2002.

Witches Abroad. HarperTorch, 2002.

Small Gods. HarperTorch, 1994.

Lords and Ladies. HarperTorch, 1996.

Men at Arms. HarperTorch, 1997.

Soul Music. HarperTorch, 2005.

Feet of Clay. HarperTorch, 2007.

Interesting Times. HarperTorch, 1998.

Maskerade. HarperTorch, 1998.

Hogfather. Harper, 1999.

Jingo. HarperTorch, 1999.

The Last Continent. HarperTorch, 2004.

Carpe Jugulum. HarperTorch, 2000.

The Fifth Elephant. HarperTorch, 2001.

The Truth. HarperTorch, 2001.

Thief of Time. HarperTorch, 2002.

Last Hero: A Discworld Fable. HarperCollins, 2001.

Night Watch. HarperTorch, 2003.

The Wee Free Men. HarperCollins, 2003.

Monstrous Regiment. HarperCollins, 2003.

A Hat Full of Sky: The Continuing Adventures of Tiffany Aching and the Wee Free Men. HarperCollins, 2004.

31 Going Postal. HarperCollins, 2004.

Wintersmith. HarperTempest, 2005.

Thud! HarperCollins, 2005.

Making Money. HarperCollins, 2007.

Unseen Academicals. HarperCollins, 2009.

Philip Pullman. His Dark Materials series.

The Golden Compass. Knopf, 1996.

The Subtle Knife. Knopf, 1997.

The Amber Spyglass. Knopf, 2000.

Ken Scholes. *Lamentation.* Tor, 2009.

Michael Scott. The Secrets of the Immortal Nicholas Flamel series.

The Alchemyst. Delacorte, 2007.

The Magician. Delacorte, 2008.

The Sorceress. Delacorte, 2009.

Rebecca Stead. *First Light.* Wendy Lamb, 2007.

Jonathan Stroud. The Bartimaeus Trilogy series.

The Amulet of Samarkand. Miramax, 2003.

The Golem's Eye. Miramax, 2004.

Ptolemy's Gate. Miramax, 2005.

J. R. R. Tolkien. The Lord of the Rings series.

The Fellowship of the Ring. Houghton Mifflin, 1988.

The Two Towers. Houghton Mifflin, 1988.

The Return of the King. Houghton Mifflin, 1988.

J. R. R. Tolkien. *The Silmarillion.* Mariner Books, 2001.

J. R. R. Tolkien and Christopher Tolkien. The History of Middle-Earth series.

The Book of Lost Tales. Houghton Mifflin, 1984.

The Book of Lost Tales, Part Two. Houghton Mifflin, 1984.

The Lays of Beleriand. Houghton Mifflin, 1985.

The Shaping of Middle-Earth: The Quenta, the Ambarkanta and the Annals. Houghton Mifflin, 1986.

The Lost Road and Other Writings. Houghton Mifflin, 1987.

The Return of the Shadow: The History of the Lord of the Rings, Part One. Houghton Mifflin, 1989.

Treason of Isengard: The History of the Lord of the Rings, Part Two. Houghton Mifflin, 1989.

The War of the Ring: The History of the Lord of the Rings, Part Three. Houghton Mifflin, 1990.

Sauron Defeated: The History of the Lord of the Rings, Part Four. Houghton Mifflin, 1992.

Morgoth's Ring: The Later Silmarillion, Part One. Houghton Mifflin, 1993.

The War of the Jewels: The Later Silmarillion, Part Two. Houghton Mifflin, 1994.

The Peoples of Middle-Earth. Houghton Mifflin, 1996.

"NO MAGIC PLEASE"

You will occasionally run into children, or their parents, who do not want any elements of magic or fantastical creatures in their reading but still want to read fantasy. Call this "realistic fantasy" if you need a label. That may seem contradictory, but there are fantasy realms that do not include any magic as well as some science fiction titles that deal with alternative histories that may fit the bill.

Jeanne DuPrau. Books of Ember series.

Rebecca Stead. *First Light*. Wendy Lamb, 2007.

David Ward. The Grassland Trilogy series.

HUMOR FANTASY

One of the earliest of the new efforts toward the mixing of genres led to fantasy that was as much about humor as the exploration of other or alternate worlds. Mixing two such boy-friendly genres cannot help but create appeal. Here are some of the best of this subgenre.

Philip Caveney. Sebastian Darke series.

David Elliott. *Jeremy Cabbage and the Living Museum of Human Oddballs and Quadruped Delights*. Knopf, 2008.

Christopher Moore. *Fluke; or, I Know Why the Winged Whale Sings*. Morrow, 2003.

Terry Pratchett. Discworld series.

Jon Scieszka. The Time Warp Trio series.

MARTIAL ARTS FANTASY

An exciting new subgenre of fantasy is works based on the martial arts. These books combine the action of combat with the mysticism of mind training. Add in magical elements and fantastical beasts, set it in the exotic climes of the Far East, and you have a formula for a gripping tale that is sure to drive the boys crazy.

Alison Goodman. *Eon: Dragoneye Reborn*. Viking, 2008.

Lian Hearn. Tales of the Otori series.

Jeff Stone. The Five Ancestors series.

BOOK LISTS FOR BOYS
Science Fiction

Science fiction for children is not nearly as common as fantasy for children, but there are books out there to be had, even for young kids. The younger the target audience is, the more the book is likely to be humorous in nature, and the more the lines blur between sci-fi and fantasy. Here are a few titles to get those future sci-fi fanatics started on the right path.

SCIENCE FICTION FOR ELEMENTARY SCHOOL BOYS

Bruce Coville. Bruce Coville's Alien Adventures series.

Aliens Ate My Homework. Minstrel, 1993.

I Left My Sneakers in Dimension X. Minstrel, 1994.

The Search for Snout. Minstrel, 1995.

Aliens Stole My Body. Minstrel, 1998.

Lawrence David. Horace Splattly series.

Horace Splattly: The Cupcaked Crusader. Puffin, 2002.

When Second Graders Attack. Puffin, 2002.

The Terror of the Pink Dodo Balloons. Puffin, 2003.

To Catch a Clownosaurus. Puffin, 2003.

The Invasion of the Shag Carpet Creature. Puffin, 2004.

The Most Evil, Friendly Villain Ever. Puffin, 2004.

David Elliott. *The Transmogrification of Roscoe Wizzle.* Candlewick, 2001.

SCIENCE FICTION FOR MIDDLE SCHOOL BOYS

Eoin Colfer. Artemis Fowl series.

Artemis Fowl. Miramax, 2001.

The Arctic Incident. Miramax, 2002.

The Eternity Code. Miramax, 2003.

The Opal Deception. Miramax, 2005.

The Lost Colony. Miramax, 2006.

The Time Paradox. Hyperion, 2008.

Jeanne DuPrau. Books of Ember series.

The City of Ember. Random House, 2003.

The People of Sparks. Random House, 2004.

The Prophet of Yonwood. Random House, 2006.

The Diamond of Darkhold. Random House, 2008.

Will Hobbs. *Go Big or Go Home.* HarperCollins, 2008.

Lois Lowry. *The Giver.* Laurel-Leaf, 2002.

SCIENCE FICTION FOR HIGH SCHOOL BOYS

M. T. Anderson. *Feed.* Candlewick, 2004.

Pete Hautman. *Rash.* Simon and Schuster, 2006.

Kenneth Oppel. *Dead Water Zone.* HarperTeen, 2007.

————. Matt Cruise series.

Airborn. HarperTeen, 2004.

Skybreaker. HarperTeen, 2007.

Starclimber. HarperTeen, 2009.

James Patterson. Maximum Ride series.

The Angel Experiment. Little, Brown, 2005.

School's Out—Forever. Warner, 2006.

Saving the World, and Other Extreme Sports. Little, Brown, 2007.

The Final Warning. Little, Brown, 2008.

Max. Little, Brown, 2009.

Rodman Philbrick. *The Last Book in the Universe.* Blue Sky, 2000.

Neal Schusterman. *Unwind.* Simon and Schuster, 2007.

Rebecca Stead. *First Light.* Wendy Lamb, 2007.

Will Weaver. *Defect.* Farrar, Strauss, and Giroux, 2007.

CHAPTER 14

BOOK LISTS FOR BOYS
Gothic Horror

All right, this is where assigning age levels is going to get me in deep water. Many of these books may make adults uncomfortable, some may seem too adult for a teen audience, but there are in fact gothic horror books designed for teens and even younger readers. Consider the more girl-oriented subgenre of gothic romance, and the popularity of series such as the Twilight Saga, by Stephenie Meyer, and realize that boys deserve the same opportunities to explore this otherworldly form. Whether you choose to offer these books to their intended audience is, of course, up to your discretion as a readers' advisor, but there are many boys who are drawn to scary stories from their earliest days around a campfire. There are also some truly funny examples of the genre, in a subgenre I like to call gothic humor, identified at the end of the list.

GOTHIC HORROR FOR ELEMENTARY SCHOOL BOYS

Dan Greenburg. Secrets of Dripping Fang series.

The Onts. Harcourt, 2005.

Treachery and Betrayal at Jolly Days. Harcourt, 2006.

The Vampire's Curse. Harcourt, 2006.

Fall of the House of Mandible. Harcourt, 2006.

The Shluffmuffin Boy Is History. Harcourt, 2006.

Attack of the Giant Octopus. Harcourt, 2007.

Please Don't Eat the Children. Harcourt, 2007.

When Bad Snakes Attack Good Children. Harcourt, 2007.

GOTHIC HORROR FOR MIDDLE SCHOOL BOYS

Joseph Delaney. The Last Apprentice series.

Revenge of the Witch. Greenwillow, 2006.

Curse of the Bane. Greenwillow, 2007.

Night of the Soul Stealer. Greenwillow, 2007.

Attack of the Fiend. Greenwillow, 2008.

Wrath of the Bloodeye. Greenwillow, 2008.

The Spook's Tale, and Other Horrors. HarperCollins, 2009.

Neil Gaiman. *The Graveyard Book*. HarperCollins, 2008.

Anthony Horowitz. Horowitz Horror series.

Night Bus. Orchard, 2008.

Killer Camera. Orchard, 2008.

The Phone Goes Dead. Orchard, 2008.

Burnt. Orchard, 2008.

Twist Cottage. Orchard, 2008.

Scared. Orchard, 2008.

Anthony Horowitz. *Horowitz Horror: Stories You'll Wish You Never Read*. Philomel, 2006.

———. *More Horowitz Horror: More Stories You'll Wish You Never Read*. Philomel, 2007.

Peg Kehret. *The Ghost's Grave*. Dutton, 2005.

Darren Shan. Cirque Du Freak: The Saga of Darren Shan series.

Cirque Du Freak: A Living Nightmare. Little, Brown, 2001.

The Vampire's Assistant. Little, Brown, 2001.

Tunnels of Blood. Little, Brown, 2002.

Vampire Mountain. Little, Brown, 2002.

Trials of Death. Little, Brown, 2003.

The Vampire Prince. Little, Brown, 2003.

Hunters of the Dusk. Little, Brown, 2004.

Allies of the Night. Little, Brown, 2004.

Killers of the Dawn. Little, Brown, 2005.

The Lake of Souls. Little, Brown, 2006.

Lord of the Shadows. Little, Brown, 2006.

Sons of Destiny. Little, Brown, 2006.

Paul Stewart and Chris Riddell. Barnaby Grimes series.

    Curse of the Night Wolf. David Fickling, 2007.

    Return of the Emerald Skull. David Fickling, 2009.

    Legion of the Dead. Doubleday, 2008.

Bram Stoker and Michael Mucci. *Dracula.* All-Action Classics. Sterling, 2007.

Brad Strickland. Lewis Barnavelt series.

    The Specter from the Magician's Museum. Dial, 1998.

    The Beast from the Wizard's Bridge. Dial, 2000.

    The Tower at the End of the World. Dial, 2001.

    The Whistle, the Grave, and the Ghost. Dial, 2003.

    The House Where Nobody Lived. Dial, 2006.

    The Sign of the Sinister Sorcerer. Dial, 2008.

Michael Teitelbaum. *The Scary States of America.* Delacorte, 2007.

Bill Wallace. *Skinny-Dipping at Monster Lake.* Simon and Schuster, 2003.

GOTHIC HORROR FOR HIGH SCHOOL BOYS

Jane Austen and Seth Grahame-Smith. *Pride and Prejudice and Zombies.* Quirk Books, 2009.

Gary Cross. *Plague of the Undead.* Puffin New Zealand, 2009.

Anthony Horowitz. The Gatekeepers series.

    Raven's Gate. Scholastic, 2005.

    Evil Star. Scholastic, 2006.

    Nightrise. Scholastic, 2007.

    Necropolis. Scholastic, 2009.

A. M. Jenkins. *Night Road.* HarperTeen, 2008.

———. *Repossessed.* HarperTeen, 2007.

Christopher Moore. *Bloodsucking Fiends.* Simon and Schuster, 1995.

———. *A Dirty Job.* William Morrow, 2006.

———. *You Suck: A Love Story.* William Morrow, 2007.

Darren Shan. The Demonata series.

    Lord Loss. Little, Brown, 2005.

    The Demon Thief. Little, Brown, 2006.

Slawter. Little, Brown, 2006.

Bec. Little, Brown, 2007.

Blood Beast. Little, Brown, 2007.

Demon Apocalypse. Little, Brown, 2007.

Death's Shadow. Little, Brown, 2008.

Wolf Island. Little, Brown, 2009.

Stephen Spignesi. *The Weird 100: A Collection of the Strange and the Unexplained.* Citadel, 2004.

Paul Zindel. *Loch.* HarperCollins, 1994.

GOTHIC HUMOR

Dan Greenburg. Secrets of Dripping Fang series.

A. M. Jenkins. *Repossessed.* HarperTeen, 2007.

Christopher Moore. *Bloodsucking Fiends.* Simon and Schuster, 1995.

———. *A Dirty Job.* William Morrow, 2006.

———. *You Suck: A Love Story.* William Morrow, 2007.

CHAPTER 15

BOOK LISTS FOR BOYS
Action, Adventure, and Mystery

This is a huge catchall category of books that get the blood pumping, ranging from the amateur detectives poking their noses where they do not belong to the boy on his own in the great outdoors. There are political thrillers, technothrillers, and anything else that tends to deal with a boy in trouble. These are mostly books about the world as we know it, even if the story itself may at times be implausible. They are plot based, which is the main distinction between these books and what we refer to as "realistic fiction" (see chapter 19, "Book Lists for Boys: Realistic Fiction").

ACTION, ADVENTURE, AND MYSTERY FOR ELEMENTARY SCHOOL BOYS

Bruce Hale. From the Tattered Casebook of Chet Gecko, Private Eye series.

The Chameleon Wore Chartreuse. Harcourt, 2000.

The Mystery of Mr. Nice. Harcourt, 2000.

Farewell, My Lunchbag. Harcourt, 2001.

The Big Nap. Harcourt, 2001.

The Hamster of the Baskervilles. Harcourt, 2002.

This Gum for Hire. Harcourt, 2002.

The Malted Falcon. Harcourt, 2003.

Trouble Is My Beeswax. Harcourt, 2003.

Give My Regrets to Broadway. Harcourt, 2004.

    Murder, My Tweet. Harcourt, 2004.

    The Possum Always Rings Twice. Harcourt, 2006.

    Key Lardo. Harcourt, 2006.

    Hiss Me Deadly. Harcourt, 2007.

    From Russia with Lunch. Harcourt, 2009.

Peter Lerangis. Abracadabra! series.

    Poof! Rabbits Everywhere! Scholastic, 2001.

    Boo! Ghosts in the School! Scholastic, 2002.

    Presto! Magic Treasure! Scholastic, 2002.

    Yeeps! Secret in the Statue! Scholastic, 2002.

    Zap! Science Fair Surprise! Scholastic, 2003.

    Yikes! It's Alive! Scholastic, 2003.

    Whoa! Amusement Park Gone Wild! Scholastic, 2003.

    Wow! Blast from the Past! Scholastic, 2003.

ACTION, ADVENTURE, AND MYSTERY FOR MIDDLE SCHOOL BOYS

The 39 Clues series.

    Rick Riordan. *Maze of Bones.* Scholastic, 2008.

    Gordon Korman. *One False Note.* Scholastic, 2008.

    Peter Lerangis. *The Sword Thief.* Scholastic, 2009.

    Jude Watson. *Beyond the Grave.* Scholastic, 2009.

Andrew Clements. *A Week in the Woods.* Simon and Schuster, 2002.

Dan Gutman. *Getting Air.* Simon and Schuster, 2007.

Sid Hite. *Stick & Whittle.* Scholastic, 2000.

Will Hobbs. *Wild Man Island.* HarperTrophy, 2002.

Anthony Horowitz. Alex Rider Adventures series.

    Stormbreaker. Philomel, 2001.

    Point Blank. Philomel, 2002.

    Skeleton Key. Philomel, 2003.

    Eagle Strike. Philomel, 2004.

    Scorpia. Philomel, 2005.

    Ark Angel. Philomel, 2006.

    Snakehead. Philomel, 2007.

Gordon Korman. Dive series.

    The Discovery. Scholastic, 2003.

    The Deep. Scholastic, 2003.

    The Danger. Scholastic, 2003.

Gordon Korman. Everest series.

    The Contest. Scholastic, 2002.

    The Climb. Scholastic, 2002.

    The Summit. Scholastic, 2002.

Gordon Korman. Island series.

    Shipwreck. Scholastic, 2001.

    Survival. Scholastic, 2001.

    Escape. Scholastic, 2001.

Gordon Korman. Kidnapped series.

    Abduction. Scholastic, 2006.

    The Search. Scholastic, 2006.

    Rescue. Scholastic, 2006.

Gordon Korman. On the Run series.

    Chasing the Falconers. Scholastic, 2005.

    The Fugitive Factor. Scholastic, 2005.

    Now You See Them, Now You Don't. Scholastic, 2005.

    The Stowaway Solution. Scholastic, 2005.

    Public Enemies. Scholastic, 2005.

    Hunting the Hunter. Scholastic, 2006.

Gordon Korman. *Swindle.* Scholastic, 2008.

Ben Mikaelsen. *Countdown.* Disney, 1996.

———. *Rescue Josh McGuire.* Hyperion, 1991.

Rodman Philbrick. *The Young Man and the Sea.* Blue Sky, 2004.

Lemony Snicket. A Series of Unfortunate Events series.

    The Bad Beginning. HarperCollins, 1999.

    The Reptile Room. HarperCollins, 1999.

    The Wide Window. HarperCollins, 2000.

    The Miserable Mill. HarperCollins, 2000.

    The Austere Academy. HarperCollins, 2000.

    The Ersatz Elevator. HarperCollins, 2001.

The Vile Village. HarperCollins, 2001.

The Hostile Hospital. HarperCollins, 2001.

The Carnivorous Carnival. HarperCollins, 2002.

The Slippery Slope. HarperCollins, 2003.

The Grim Grotto. HarperCollins, 2004.

The Penultimate Peril. HarperCollins, 2005.

The End. HarperCollins, 2006.

Wendelin Van Draanen. The Gecko and Sticky series.

Villain's Lair. Knopf, 2009.

The Greatest Power. Knopf, 2009.

Wendelin Van Draanen. Shredderman series.

Secret Identity. Knopf, 2004.

Attack of the Tagger. Knopf, 2004.

Meet the Gecko. Knopf, 2005.

Enemy Spy. Knopf, 2005.

ACTION, ADVENTURE, AND MYSTERY FOR HIGH SCHOOL BOYS

Isabel Allende. *City of the Beasts.* Rayo, 2002.

Joseph Bruchac. *Bearwalker.* HarperCollins, 2007.

Stephen Cole. *Thieves like Us.* Bloomsbury, 2006.

———. *Thieves till We Die.* Bloomsbury, 2007.

Ben Mikaelsen. *Touching Spirit Bear.* HarperCollins, 2001.

———. *Ghost of Spirit Bear.* HarperCollins, 2008.

Gary Paulsen. *The Car.* Harcourt Brace, 1994.

Graham Salisbury. *Night of the Howling Dogs.* Wendy Lamb, 2007.

Todd Strasser. Drift X series.

Slide or Die. Simon Pulse, 2006.

Battle Drift. Simon Pulse, 2006.

Sidewayz Glory. Simon Pulse, 2006.

Mark Walden. H.I.V.E. series.

H.I.V.E.: The Higher Institute of Villainous Education. Simon and Schuster, 2007.

The Overlord Protocol. Simon and Schuster, 2008.

CHAPTER 16

BOOK LISTS FOR BOYS
Sports

Books about sports are an important way to reach boys. Too often, we deny the connection between mind and body, but boys are physical creatures, and they like to read about people doing things that they enjoy. For many years we had few sports books for children, and the ones we had tended to be more about personal growth and morality lessons than the games themselves. The best of today's sports stories focus on the sports, with plenty of action and suspense.

SPORTS BOOKS FOR ELEMENTARY SCHOOL BOYS

Matt Christopher. Soccer Cats series. [Soccer]
>*The Captain Contest.* Little, Brown, 1999.
>*Operation Babysitter.* Little, Brown, 1999.
>*Secret Weapon.* Little, Brown, 2000.
>*Hat Trick.* Little, Brown, 2000.
>*Master of Disaster.* Little, Brown, 2001.
>*Heads Up.* Little, Brown, 2001.
>*All Keyed Up.* Little, Brown, 2002.
>*You Lucky Dog.* Little, Brown, 2002.

Dan Gutman. Baseball Card Mysteries series. [Baseball]
>*Honus & Me.* HarperCollins, 1997.
>*Jackie & Me.* HarperCollins, 1999.
>*Babe & Me.* HarperCollins, 2000.

Shoeless Joe & Me. HarperCollins, 2002.

Mickey & Me. HarperCollins, 2003.

Abner & Me. HarperCollins, 2005.

Satch & Me. HarperCollins, 2006.

Jim & Me. HarperCollins, 2008.

Ray & Me. HarperCollins, 2009.

Mike Lupica. Mike Lupica's Comeback Kids series.

Hot Hand. Philomel, 2007. [Basketball]

Long Shot. Philomel, 2008. [Basketball]

Safe at Home. Philomel, 2008. [Baseball]

Two-Minute Drill. Philomel, 2007. [Football]

Ken Roberts. *Thumb on a Diamond.* Groundwood, 2006. [Baseball]

SPORTS BOOKS FOR MIDDLE SCHOOL BOYS

John Feinstein. *Cover-Up: Mystery at the Super Bowl.* Knopf, 2007. [Football]

———. *Last Shot: A Final Four Mystery.* Knopf, 2005. [Basketball]

———. *Vanishing Act: Mystery at the U.S. Open.* Knopf, 2006. [Tennis]

Tim Green. *Baseball Great.* HarperCollins, 2009. [Baseball]

———. *Football Champ.* HarperCollins, 2009. [Football]

———. *Football Genius.* HarperCollins, 2007. [Football]

———. *Football Hero.* HarperCollins, 2008. [Football]

Dan Gutman. *The Secret Life of Doctor Demented.* Simon Pulse, 2001. [Wrestling]

Gordon Korman. *The Chicken Doesn't Skate.* Scholastic, 1996. [Hockey]

Mike Lupica. *The Big Field.* Penguin, 2008. [Baseball]

———. *Heat.* Philomel, 2006. [Baseball]

———. *Travel Team.* Philomel, 2004. [Basketball]

Chris Lynch. *Gold Dust.* HarperCollins, 2000. [Baseball]

Kadir Nelson. *We Are the Ship: The Story of Negro League Baseball.* Jump at the Sun, 2008. [Baseball, Nonfiction]

Gary Paulsen. *How Angel Peterson Got His Name, and Other Outrageous Tales of Extreme Sports.* Yearling, 2004. [Extreme Sports]

John H. Ritter. *The Boy Who Saved Baseball*. Philomel, 2003. [Baseball]

Timothy Tocher. *Chief Sunrise, John McGraw, and Me*. Cricket, 2004.
    [Baseball]

SPORTS BOOKS FOR HIGH SCHOOL BOYS

Carl Deuker. *Gym Candy*. Houghton Mifflin, 2007. [Football]

John Grisham. *Playing for Pizza*. Doubleday, 2007. [Football]

Michael Lewis. *The Blind Side: Evolution of a Game*. Norton, 2007.
    [Football, Nonfiction]

Alfred C. Martino. *Over the End Line*. Houghton Mifflin, 2009. [Soccer]

———. *Pinned*. Harcourt, 2005. [Wrestling]

Walter Dean Myers. *Game*. HarperTeen, 2008. [Basketball]

———. *Hoops*. Delacorte, 1991. [Basketball]

———. *The Outside Shot*. Delacorte, 1984. [Basketball]

———. *Slam!* Scholastic, 1996. [Basketball]

David Skuy. *Off the Crossbar*. Writer's Collective, 2006. [Hockey]

CHAPTER 17

BOOK LISTS FOR BOYS
Visual Storytelling

O ne of the reasons so many boys who were so into books as preschoolers become nonreaders by their mid-elementary years is that we take the pictures out of their reading. Illustrations stimulate the whole brain and give visual clues that help the struggling reader to understand more complex and engaging story lines. Still, our society seems to have a bias against illustrated works. That is changing with the advent of relatively new visual formats and the reinvention of some old ones. We start with the classic picture books for those preschool boys, then go on to all kinds of visual storytelling. Boys today can have their pictures and read them too, right through their teen years.

PICTURE BOOKS FOR BOYS

Carolyn Buehner. *Superdog: The Heart of a Hero.* HarperCollins, 2003.

Julia Donaldson. *The Gruffalo.* Dial, 1999.

Kristine O'Connell George. Illustrated by Laura Stringer. *Fold Me a Poem.* Harcourt, 2005.

Marty Kelley. *The Rules.* Knowledge Unlimited, 2000.

———. *Twelve Terrible Things.* Tricycle Press, 2008.

David Martin. *Piggy and Dad Go Fishing.* Candlewick, 2005.

Kate McMullan. *I Stink!* Joanna Cotler, 2002.

Mary Elise Monsell. *Underwear!* Whitman, 1988.

Dav Pilkey. *Dog Breath: The Horrible Trouble with Hally Tosis.* Blue Sky, 1994.

————. *Dogzilla.* Harcourt, 1993.

————. *Kat Kong.* Harcourt, 1993.

Jon Scieszka. *The Stinky Cheese Man and Other Fairly Stupid Tales.* Viking, 1993.

————. *The True Story of the Three Little Pigs.* Viking, 1989.

David Shannon. *No, David!* Scholastic, 1998.

Judy Sierra. Pictures by Stephen Gammell. *The Secret Science Project That Almost Ate the School.* Simon and Schuster, 2007.

Erik John Slangerup. *Dirt Boy.* Sagebrush, 2003.

David Wiesner. *Sector 7.* Houghton Mifflin, 1999.

————. *The Three Pigs.* Clarion, 2001.

————. *Tuesday.* Clarion, 1991.

Janet S. Wong. Illustrated by Stacey Schuett. *Alex and the Wednesday Chess Club.* Margaret K. McElderry, 2004.

NONFICTION PICTURE BOOKS

True books for the little guys have always been a haven for boy readers. The most stereotypical of these books involve trucks, ships, planes, dinosaurs, snakes, and creepy crawlies; they are legion and have lasting appeal. Add to these some of the more boy-focused titles listed below, and you are well on your way. These titles include, also, some great books to suggest when you have an older boy who will read to a younger boy. The picture-book format is so powerful that it has appeal years after the boy has grown past it, and it constitutes a safe and comfortable platform for the older struggling reader.

Karen Chin and Thom Holmes. *Dino Dung: The Scoop on Fossil Feces.* Random House, 2004.

Susan E. Goodman. Illustrated by Elwood H. Smith. *The Truth about Poop.* Viking, 2004.

Robert Gould. Big Stuff series.

    Monster Trucks. Big Guy Books, 2004.

    Tractors. Big Guy Books, 2004.

    Big Rigs. Big Guy Books, 2004.

    Giant Earthmovers. Big Guy Books, 2004.

    Rescue Vehicles. Big Guy Books, 2005.

Racers. Big Guy Books, 2005.

Sea Creatures. Big Guy Books, 2005.

Dinosaurs. Big Guy Books, 2005.

Kathleen Kudlinski. *Boy, Were We Wrong about Dinosaurs!* Dutton, 2005.

Marilyn Singer. *What Stinks?* Darby Creek, 2006.

ILLUSTRATED BOOKS, COMICS, GRAPHIC NOVELS, AND MANGA FOR ELEMENTARY SCHOOL BOYS

Erik Craddock. Stone Rabbit series. [Graphic Novels]

B.C. Mambo. Random House, 2009.

Pirate Palooza. Random House, 2009.

Deep Space Disco. Random House, 2009.

Kathleen Duey. Time Soldiers series.

Rex. Big Guy Books, 2000.

Rex 2. Big Guy Books, 2000.

Patch. Big Guy Books, 2002.

Arthur. Big Guy Books, 2004.

Mummy. Big Guy Books, 2005.

Samurai. Big Guy Books, 2006.

Pony Express. Big Guy Books, 2006.

Jarrett J. Krosoczka. Lunch Lady series.

Lunch Lady and the Cyborg Substitute. Knopf, 2009.

Lunch Lady and the League of Librarians. Knopf, 2009.

Sandra Markle. *Outside and Inside Mummies.* Walker, 2005. [Nonfiction]

Walter Dean Myers. *Patrol: An American Soldier in Vietnam.* HarperCollins, 2002.

Dav Pilkey. Captain Underpants series.

The Adventures of Captain Underpants: An Epic Novel. Little Apple, 1997.

Captain Underpants and the Attack of the Talking Toilets. Little Apple, 1999.

Captain Underpants and the Invasion of the Incredibly Naughty Cafeteria Ladies from Outer Space (and the Subsequent Assault of Equally Evil Lunchroom Zombie Nerds). Little Apple, 1999.

Captain Underpants and the Perilous Plot of Professor Poopypants. Blue Sky, 2000.

Captain Underpants and the Wrath of the Wicked Wedgie Woman. Blue Sky, 2001.

Captain Underpants Extra-Crunchy Book o' Fun. Blue Sky, 2001.

The All New Captain Underpants Extra-Crunchy Book o' Fun 2. Blue Sky, 2002.

The Adventures of Super Diaper Baby. Blue Sky, 2002.

Captain Underpants and the Big, Bad Battle of the Bionic Booger Boy, Part 1: The Night of the Nasty Nostril Nuggets. Blue Sky, 2003.

Captain Underpants and the Big, Bad Battle of the Bionic Booger Boy, Part 2: Revenge of the Ridiculous Robo-Boogers. Blue Sky, 2003.

Captain Underpants and the Preposterous Plight of the Purple Potty People. Scholastic, 2006.

Dav Pilkey. Illustrated by Martin Ontiveros. Ricky Ricotta series.

Ricky Ricotta's Giant Robot. Blue Sky, 2000.

Ricky Ricotta's Mighty Robot vs. the Mutant Mosquitoes from Mercury. Blue Sky, 2000.

Ricky Ricotta's Mighty Robot vs. the Voodoo Vultures from Venus. Blue Sky, 2001.

Ricky Ricotta's Mighty Robot vs. the Mecha-Monkeys from Mars. Blue Sky, 2002.

Ricky Ricotta's Mighty Robot vs. the Jurassic Jackrabbits from Jupiter. Blue Sky, 2002.

Ricky Ricotta's Mighty Robot vs. the Stupid Stinkbugs from Saturn. Blue Sky, 2003.

Ricky Ricotta's Mighty Robot vs. the Uranium Unicorns from Uranus. Blue Sky, 2005.

Hudson Talbott. *Safari Journal: The Adventures in Africa of Carey Monroe.* Silver Whistle, 2003.

ILLUSTRATED BOOKS, COMICS, GRAPHIC NOVELS, AND MANGA FOR MIDDLE SCHOOL BOYS

All-Action Classics series. [Graphic Novels]

Bram Stoker and Michael Mucci. *Dracula.* Sterling, 2007.

Mark Twain, Tim Mucci, and Rad Sechrist. *Tom Sawyer.* Sterling, 2007.

Frank Cammuso. Knights of the Lunch Table series. [Graphic Novels]

    The Dodgeball Chronicles. Scholastic, 2008.

    The Dragon Players. Scholastic, 2009.

Ricardo Delgado. Age of Reptiles series. [Graphic Novels]

    Tribal Warfare. Dark Horse Comics, 1993.

    The Hunt. Dark Horse Comics, 1997.

Paul Fleisher. *Parasites: Latching On to a Free Lunch.* Twenty-First Century Books, 2006. [Nonfiction]

Jeff Kinney. Diary of a Wimpy Kid series.

    Diary of a Wimpy Kid. Amulet, 2007.

    Diary of a Wimpy Kid: Rodrick Rules. Amulet, 2008.

    Diary of a Wimpy Kid: Do-It-Yourself Book. Amulet, 2008.

    Diary of a Wimpy Kid: The Last Straw. Amulet, 2009.

Jeff Smith. Bone series. [Comic Books]

    Out from Boneville. Scholastic, 2005.

    The Great Cow Race. Graphix, 2005.

    Eyes of the Storm. Graphix, 2006.

    The Dragonslayer. Graphix, 2006.

    Rock Jaw: Master of the Eastern Border. Graphix, 2007.

    Old Man's Cave. Graphix, 2007.

    Ghost Circles. Graphix, 2008.

    Treasure Hunters. Graphix, 2008.

    Crown of Horns. Graphix, 2009.

Jeff Smith. *Bone: The Complete Epic in One Volume.* Cartoon Books, 2004. [Comic Books]

Andrew Solway. *What's Living in Your Bedroom?* Heinemann, 2004. [Nonfiction]

ILLUSTRATED BOOKS, COMICS, GRAPHIC NOVELS, AND MANGA FOR HIGH SCHOOL BOYS

Ken Akamatsu. *Negima! Master Negi Magi.* Del Rey, 2004–. [Manga]

Neil Gaiman, John Bolton, Scott Hampton, and Charles Vess. *The Books of Magic.* DC Comics, 1993. [Graphic Novel]

Matsuri Hino. *Vampire Knight.* Shojo Beat, 2007–. [Manga]

Satomi Ikezawa. *Othello.* Del Rey, 2004–. [Manga]

Dean Koontz and Queenie Chan. *In Odd We Trust.* Ballantine, 2008. [Graphic Novel]

Roland Laird and Taneshia Nash Laird. *Still I Rise: A Graphic History of African Americans.* Sterling, 2009. [Graphic Novel, Nonfiction]

Mahiro Maeda and Yura Ariwara. *Gankutsuou: The Count of Monte Cristo.* Ballantine, 2008–. [Manga]

Mitsukazu Mihara. *Haunted House.* TokyoPop, 2006. [Manga]

James Patterson. *Daniel X: Alien Hunter.* Little, Brown, 2008. [Graphic Novel]

William Shakespeare. Illustrated by Emma Vieceli. *Hamlet: Prince of Denmark.* Manga Shakespeare series. Abrams, 2007. [Manga]

————. Illustrated by Sonia Leong. *Romeo and Juliet.* Manga Shakespeare series. Amulet, 2007. [Manga]

Sue Stauffacher. *Wireman.* Sue Stauffacher, 2005–2006. [Comic Books]

Yukiru Sugisaki. *D. N. Angel.* TokyoPop, 2004–. [Manga]

Yoshihiro Togashi. *YuYu Hakusho.* VIZ Media, 2003–. [Manga]

Naoki Urasawa. *20th Century Boys.* VIZ Media, 2009–. [Manga]

Joss Whedon, Karl Moline, and Andy Owens. *Fray.* Dark Horse Comics, 2003. [Graphic Novel]

Futaro Yamada and Masaki Segawa. *Basilisk.* Del Rey, 2006–. [Manga]

CHAPTER 18

BOOK LISTS FOR BOYS

Historical Fiction

H istorical fiction is often thought of as a boy-friendly genre because of the number of males who like to read history. But many boys would rather just read history than historical fiction. Most historical fiction uses the historical setting as an interesting backdrop, a way to put characters in context. The historical fiction titles that appeal most to boys are the ones that use the historical setting as a plot element. Here are just a few recent titles that may speak best to boys.

Avi. *Crispin: Cross of Lead.* Hyperion, 2002.

Christopher Paul Curtis. *The Watsons Go to Birmingham.* Delacorte, 1995.

Chris Lynch. *Gold Dust.* HarperCollins, 2000.

Andrew Matthews. *The Way of the Warrior.* Dutton, 2008.

Gary Paulsen. *The Rifle.* Harcourt Brace, 1995.

WAR STORIES

Joseph Bruchac. *Code Talker: A Novel about the Navajo Marines of World War Two.* Speak, 2005.

Harry Mazer. *A Boy at War: A Novel of Pearl Harbor.* Simon and Schuster, 2001.

———. *A Boy No More.* Simon and Schuster, 2004.

Walter Dean Myers. *Patrol: An American Soldier in Vietnam.* HarperCollins, 2002.

Roland Smith. *Elephant Run.* Hyperion, 2007.

CHAPTER 19

BOOK LISTS FOR BOYS
Realistic Fiction

Realistic fiction might be the most euphemistically named genre in literature. When we use it, we are mostly talking about issue books in the classic form of the juvenile novel, and it seems the more depressing, the more unusual the circumstances, the better. The format is usually more geared toward the girl reader, but these books do not need to be all about long cell-phone conversations about boys and eating disorders. Realistic fiction deals with, well, real life, and life can be a story. Although these books are almost necessarily issue based and explore youth and their problems, the ones I have chosen represent a more boy-centered approach. Most will have male central characters and strong plot elements that keep them from being entirely inwardly focused. Many bring humor to play even in the most desperate of personal disasters. There is no division into age groups for these books; they are almost by definition teen books because they deal primarily with the period of life we call "coming-of-age." The list is selective, meaning very short, but can be a starting point, especially for that dreaded twelfth-grade English assignment to find a "realistic fiction" title.

Avi. *Nothing but the Truth: A Documentary Novel.* Orchard, 1991.

John Green. *An Abundance of Katherines.* Dutton, 2006.

Pete Hautman. *Godless.* Simon and Schuster, 2004.

Gordon Korman. *Jake Reinvented.* Hyperion, 2003.

———. *The Juvie Three.* Hyperion, 2008.

Walter Dean Myers. *Handbook for Boys.* Amistad, 2002.

———. *Monster.* Amistad, 1999.

————. *Shooter.* Amistad, 2004.

————. *Sunrise over Fallujah.* Scholastic, 2008.

Gary Paulsen. *The Car.* Harcourt Brace, 1994.

Jerry Spinelli. *Maniac Magee.* Little, Brown, 1990.

Todd Strasser. *Boot Camp.* Simon and Schuster, 2007.

————. *Give a Boy a Gun.* Simon Pulse, 2002.

————. *If I Grow Up.* Simon and Schuster, 2009.

————. *The Wave.* Laurel-Leaf, 1981.

Richard Uhlig. *Boy minus Girl.* Knopf, 2008.

Ned Vizzini. *It's Kind of a Funny Story.* Hyperion, 2006.

Jake Wizner. *Spanking Shakespeare.* Random House, 2007.

CHAPTER 20

CLASSIC RETELLINGS

Often, students are given great books for which they are just not ready. Here are some classic titles, and retellings in modern times. These are not simply rewritten works, or simplified versions. Neither are they stories inspired by the original, as *The Mists of Avalon,* by Marion Zimmer Bradley, builds on the Arthurian legend. These are modern takes on the original story that change the context and make the stories themselves more approachable for modern youth.

Jane Austen and Seth Grahame-Smith. *Pride and Prejudice and Zombies.* Quirk Books, 2009. [Retelling of *Pride and Prejudice,* by Jane Austen]

Jane Austen in a book list for boys? Maybe not so strange as zombies infesting the world of *Pride and Prejudice.* The original is in there, but like a real zombie, it has come back from the dead to terrorize . . . well, English teachers.

Frank Cammuso. *The Dodgeball Chronicles.* Knights of the Lunch Table series. Scholastic, 2008. [Retelling of *The Story of King Arthur and His Knights,* by Howard Pyle]

This graphic-novel, modern-day adaptation of the King Arthur legend, starring Arthur King, may seem like a silly parody, but all the heroism and mysticism of the original is there, complete with "The Ladies of Lunch"; a Yoda-like science teacher named Merlin; and the big, bad enemy, named Joe Roman. Who says you cannot be a hero on the playground?

Neil Gaiman. *The Graveyard Book.* **HarperCollins, 2008. [Retelling of** *The Jungle Book,* **by Rudyard Kipling]**

The powerful message of the original was that the jungle was the safe place; it was civilization that was the dark and scary world. Gaiman makes the point in modern terms that the world of ghosts and ghouls is ultimately less frightening than the human world.

Gordon Korman. *Jake Reinvented.* **Hyperion, 2003. [Retelling of** *The Great Gatsby,* **by F. Scott Fitzgerald]**

What is the modern equivalent of the flapper parties of the 1920s? The high school football parties. Korman takes the social pressures and feelings of social isolation, the background themes of Fitzgerald's work, and updates them to highlight the universal themes of love and longing.

Mahiro Maeda and Yura Ariwara. *Gankutsuou: The Count of Monte Cristo.* **Ballantine, 2008. [Retelling of** *The Count of Monte Cristo,* **by Alexandre Dumas]**

Maeda and Ariwara set the story in a futuristic, interplanetary world of traditional sophistication and wild worlds on the edge of the known universe, a fitting counterpart to Dumas' civilized Europe and wild lands on the edge of civilization.

Christopher Moore. *Fool.* **William Morrow, 2009. [Retelling of** *King Lear,* **by William Shakespeare]**

This retelling of Shakespeare's *King Lear* is laced with vile language, and every page has graphic references to the most perverse sex. It is completely inappropriate for any high school library, but not nearly as inappropriate as assigning a whole class of teenagers to read *King Lear.* Reading this book is like getting back at all those horrid assignments of books that were too long, too old, or just assigned at the absolute wrong time in life. I love *King Lear,* and I know this is not really a book you would give to a teen, but I would much rather have read this in high school than the original.

Michael Mucci. *Dracula.* **All-Action Classics series. Sterling, 2007. [Retelling of** *Dracula,* **by Bram Stoker]**

It is truly amazing how tight and action packed the plot of this gothic classic is—and how much of the original is devoted to description. After all, Stoker was describing lands and monsters we have not seen. Mucci's rendering uses the graphic elements as effectively as any I've seen to portray all the descriptive elements necessary to the book, freeing up the plot and making this a quick and exciting read.

Rodman Philbrick. *The Young Man and the Sea.* **Blue Sky, 2004.**
[Retelling of *The Old Man and the Sea,* **by Ernest Hemingway]**

How much easier it is to see the human struggle behind Hemingway's work when one realizes that *The Old Man and the Sea* is an adventure story. Philbrick brings out the adventure in his modern retake while respecting the great themes of the original. Any boy who reads *The Young Man and the Sea* will be more able, and much more willing, to tackle *The Old Man and the Sea.*

William Shakespeare. Illustrated by Sonia Leong. *Romeo and*
Juliet. **Manga Shakespeare series. Amulet, 2007. [Retelling**
of *Romeo and Juliet,* **by William Shakespeare]**

Part of Shakespeare's genius was that he spoke to the universal, to themes that were undying while his characters were, well, dying. How fitting, then, to take his classic love story out of the tights-wearing crowds of Renaissance Italy and drop it into the cool streets and punked-up rides of the modern Japanese teenager. After all, both cultures have a rich history of swordplay.

Michael Sullivan. *Escapade Johnson and the Phantom of the Science*
Fair. **Escapade Johnson series. PublishingWorks, 2009. [Retelling**
of *The Phantom of the Opera,* **by Gaston Leroux]**

Although the modern schoolboy may be shocked that they made a book out of the movie, the book, of course, came first. Andrew Lloyd Webber brought out the romance and heroism of the original in ways Leroux might have found surprising. I have gone after the mystery and the humor. Frankly, Leroux might have been appalled.

CHAPTER 21

GREAT AUTHORS FOR BOYS

There are some authors, within genres and across them, who consistently produce books with strong boy appeal, often at a number of age levels. It is worth mentioning them directly to simplify the process of providing readers' advisory to boys. These are authors you can reach for on a regular basis when stumped by a reluctant reader or when you do not have the opportunity to do a full readers' advisory interview.

ACTION, ADVENTURE, AND MYSTERY

Dan Gutman
Will Hobbs
Gordon Korman
Ben Mikaelsen
Gary Paulsen

Ben Mikaelsen is really the dean of the action and adventure writers. His books' appeal is mostly in how true the story rings. Mikaelsen has done all the things he writes about, from going to space camp to raising a bear from cub to full-grown adult. Gordon Korman's adventure stories often come in trilogies, thus leaving a next book for the hooked reader. Dan Gutman and Will Hobbs write accessible, enjoyable action reads, while Gary Paulsen is more cerebral and literary.

FANTASY

Piers Anthony
Terry Brooks
David Eddings
John Flanagan
Terry Pratchett
Philip Pullman
Jonathan Stroud
J. R. R. Tolkien

This category includes a number of primarily adult authors, such as J. R. R. Tolkien and Terry Brooks, to whom you can eventually steer the boys. Most of fantasy deals with universal issues, and most high fantasy is devoid of issues of sexuality, making it a great entry point for teen boys who want to reach into the adult collection. The exceptions to this rule are legendary, and you might want to be careful with Piers Anthony, for example, whose works vary from high fantasy to some pretty edgy material. John Flanagan and Jonathan Stroud are the newcomers on the list, but look for them to have long-standing success.

GOTHIC HORROR

Joseph Delaney
Anthony Horowitz
Christopher Moore
Darren Shan

More often associated with the action and adventure genre and his Alex Rider Adventures series, Anthony Horowitz is accomplished at the deeply mythological side of gothic horror. Christopher Moore's books are a humorous take on the genre, but his works can contain very edgy language and descriptions of sexuality.

HUMOR

D. L. Garfinkle
Gordon Korman
Christopher Moore

Dav Pilkey

Jon Scieszka

Christopher Moore writes humor in any number of forms; hence, his works will fall under fantasy, gothic horror, and social satire, but always, the focus of the work is humor. Similarly, Jon Scieszka writes picture books as well as fantasy, but it is always about the laughs. Gary Paulsen may be an author you may think of more as an adventure writer in the outdoor tradition, so he is not really worthy of this list, but he needs to be considered as a humor writer as well.

REALISTIC FICTION

Gordon Korman

Walter Dean Myers

Todd Strasser

Chris Crutcher

Although realistic fiction is not generally considered a boy-friendly genre, there are a few masters of the form who speak directly to boys, such as Walter Dean Myers and Todd Strasser. Chris Crutcher is often thought of as a sportswriter, and though many of his books involve sports, the focus is always on contemporary social issues, so he belongs here. Gordon Korman belongs in many categories, but whether he is trying to be funny, exciting, or acerbic, his works tend to be contemporary and relatable.

SCIENCE FICTION

Eoin Colfer

Bruce Coville

Kenneth Oppel

Though science fiction is overshadowed by and often blurred with the fantasy genre, there are some science fiction titles directed toward children. Bruce Coville has written some of the best in the realm of humorous science fiction. With the blending of technology and magic, Eoin Colfer's work often exemplifies the difficulty in categorizing science fiction in children's literature. Kenneth Oppel is closer to the classical form and is an excellent stepping-stone toward mainstream adult science fiction.

SPORTS

Carl Deuker
John Feinstein
Tim Green
Mike Lupica
Alfred C. Martino

Mike Lupica writes of the personal side of sports, focusing on young amateur athletes and their love of the game, often connecting the lessons learned on the sports field with the challenges of life. His fellow sports reporter John Feinstein takes the opposite tack—looking at the big show, the big business, and the big hype of sports—and writes about the people who ruin the game for the people who Lupica writes about loving the game. Tim Green and Alfred C. Martino are relatively new to writing, but they bring the authenticity of athletes to the genre. Green played in the National Football League, and Martino was a top-shelf high school wrestler.

CHAPTER 22

READ–ALIKES

What to give them next, when they really liked what they last read.

READ–ALIKES FOR ELEMENTARY SCHOOL BOYS

If he liked David Shannon's *No, David!* try . . .

Erik John Slangerup. *Dirt Boy.* Sagebrush, 2003.

If he liked dinosaur books when he was five, try . . .

Karen Chin and Thom Holmes. *Dino Dung: The Scoop on Fossil Feces.* Random House, 2004.

If he liked Dav Pilkey's Captain Underpants series, try . . .

Susan E. Goodman. Illustrated by Elwood H. Smith. *The Truth about Poop.* Viking, 2004.

Andy Griffiths. *The Day My Butt Went Psycho.* Scholastic, 2003.

Erik P. Kraft. Lenny and Mel series.

Pam Smallcomb. *The Last Burp of Mac McGerp.* Bloomsbury, 2004.

If he liked Jeff Kinney's Diary of a Wimpy Kid series, try . . .

Jerry Spinelli. *Loser.* Joanna Cotler, 2002.

Todd Strasser. *Is That a Dead Dog in Your Locker?* Scholastic, 2008.

If he liked Jon Scieszka's Time Warp Trio series, try . . .

Todd Strasser. Help! I'm Trapped . . . series.

Kathleen Duey. Time Soldiers series.

READ-ALIKES FOR MIDDLE SCHOOL BOYS

If he liked dinosaur books when he was five, try . . .

- Thomas R. Holtz and Luis V. Rey. *Dinosaurs: The Most Complete, Up-to-Date Encyclopedia for Dinosaur Lovers of All Ages.* Random House, 2007.

If he liked J. K. Rowling's Harry Potter series, try . . .

Emily Drake. The Magickers series.

Rick Riordan. Percy Jackson and the Olympians series.

J. K. Rowling. *Fantastic Beasts and Where to Find Them.* Scholastic, 2001.

J. K. Rowling. *Quidditch through the Ages.* Scholastic, 2001.

J. K. Rowling. *The Tales of Beedle the Bard.* Children's High Level Group, 2008.

If he likes J. R. R. Tolkien, or would like to read him someday, try . . .

John Flanagan. Ranger's Apprentice series.

Emily Rodda. Deltora Quest series.

If he liked Eoin Colfer's Artemis Fowl series, try . . .

Mark Walden. H.I.V.E. series.

If he liked *Ripley's Believe It or Not,* try . . .

Stephen Spignesi. *The Weird 100: A Collection of the Strange and the Unexplained.* Citadel, 2004.

If he loves *WWF Magazine,* try . . .

Dan Gutman. *The Secret Life of Doctor Demented.* Simon Pulse, 2001.

READ-ALIKES FOR HIGH SCHOOL BOYS

If he liked John Fleischman's *Phineas Gage,* try . . .

Ken Silverstein. *The Radioactive Boy Scout: The True Story of a Boy and His Backyard Nuclear Reactor.* Random House, 2004.

If he liked J. K. Rowling's Harry Potter series, try . . .

Ken Akamatsu. *Negima! Master Negi Magi.* Del Rey, 2004–. [Manga]

David Colbert. *The Magical Worlds of Harry Potter.* Lumina, 2001.

Roger Highfield. *The Science of Harry Potter: How Magic Really Works.* Viking, 2002.

Allan Zola Kronzek. *The Sorcerer's Companion: A Guide to the Magical World of Harry Potter.* Broadway, 2001.

Michael Scott. The Secrets of the Immortal Nicholas Flamel series.

If he loved J. R. R. Tolkien, try . . .

David Eddings. The Tamuli series.

P. R. Moredun. The World of Eldaterra series.

If he liked Philip Pullman's His Dark Materials series, try . . .

Kathleen Duey. A Resurrection of Magic series.

Nancy Farmer. *The House of the Scorpion.* Atheneum, 2002.

Jonathan Stroud. The Bartimaeus Trilogy series.

If he liked Anthony Horowitz's Alex Rider Adventures series, try . . .

Stephen Cole. *Thieves like Us.* Bloomsbury, 2006.

If he liked James Patterson's Maximum Ride series, try . . .

Kenneth Oppel. *Dead Water Zone.* HarperTeen, 2007.

Neal Schusterman. *Unwind.* Simon and Schuster, 2007.

Will Weaver. *Defect.* Farrar, Strauss, and Giroux, 2007.

If he liked Jeanne DuPrau's Books of Ember series, try . . .

Kenneth Oppel. Matt Cruise series.

Rebecca Stead. *First Light.* Wendy Lamb, 2007.

If he liked Lois Lowry's *The Giver,* try . . .

Rodman Philbrick. *The Last Book in the Universe.* Blue Sky, 2000.

If he liked Walter Dean Myers's *Monster,* try . . .

Stanley "Tookie" Williams. *Life in Prison.* Chronicle, 2001.

If he loved the TV show *Buffy the Vampire Slayer,* try . . .

Joss Whedon, Karl Moline, and Andy Owens. *Fray.* Dark Horse Comics, 2003. [Graphic Novel]

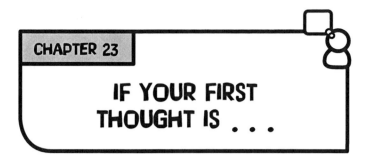

CHAPTER 23

IF YOUR FIRST THOUGHT IS . . .

Often, we are aware of boys' literature and either have an outdated view of it or try to go halfway, giving a boy a book that has some aspects that appeal to him but is limited by our own views or comfort level. Sometimes these books are in the wrong genre, sometimes they are aimed at a different audience, sometimes they are dated, and sometimes we give them to boys at the wrong stage of their lives. If you find boys lukewarm about your suggestions, allow me to offer these translations.

BETTER OPTIONS FOR ELEMENTARY SCHOOL BOYS

If your first thought is R. L. Stine's Goosebumps series, try . . .

Dan Greenburg. Secrets of Dripping Fang series.

If a boy wants sports, and your first thought is Matt Christopher . . .

try Mike Lupica.

If your first thought is A. A. Milne's *Winnie the Pooh,* try . . .

Jon Scieszka. *Summer Reading Is Killing Me.* The Time Warp Trio series. Viking, 1998.

If you start to pick up David J. Sobol's Encyclopedia Brown series, try . . .

Bruce Hale. From the Tattered Casebook of Chet Gecko, Private Eye series.

BETTER OPTIONS FOR MIDDLE SCHOOL BOYS

If your first thought is R. L. Stine's Goosebumps series, try . . .
   Darren Shan. Cirque Du Freak series.
If your first thought is R. L. Stine's Fear Street series, try . . .
   Joseph Delaney. The Last Apprentice series.
If your first thought is Jack London . . .
   try Will Hobbs.
If your first thought is Tamora Pierce, try . . .
   John Flanagan. Ranger's Apprentice series.
If your first thought is Wilson Rawls's *Where the Red Fern Grows,* try . . .
   Gordon Korman. *No More Dead Dogs.* Hyperion, 2002.
If your first thought is Mary Rodgers's *Freaky Friday,* try . . .
   Blake Nelson. *Gender Blender.* Delacorte, 2006.
If he is too young for Arthur Conan Doyle's Sherlock Holmes series,
   try . . .
   Paul Stewart and Chris Riddell. Barnaby Grimes series.
If you really loved Fred Gipson's *Old Yeller* when *you* were a boy, try . . .
   Ben Mikaelsen. *Rescue Josh Maguire.* Hyperion, 1991.
If you need a Newbery Award winner and you reach for Susan Patron's
   The Higher Power of Lucky . . .
   reach for Neil Gaiman's *The Graveyard Book* (HarperCollins, 2008)
      instead.
If you are thinking about giving him Mark Twain's *Adventures of Tom
   Sawyer* . . .
   give him Wendelin Van Draanen's *Swear to Howdy* (Knopf, 2003)
      instead.
If you are thinking of Esther Forbes's *Johnny Tremain* . . .
   Harry Mazer's *A Boy at War: A Novel of Pearl Harbor* (Simon and
      Schuster, 2001) is a better bet.

BETTER OPTIONS FOR HIGH SCHOOL BOYS

If your first thought is R. L. Stine's Fear Street series, try . . .
   Darren Shan. The Demonata series.

If your first thought is Herman Melville's *Moby Dick,* try . . .

> Nathaniel Philbrick. *Revenge of the Whale: The True Story of the Whaleship* Essex. Putnam, 2002.

If your first thought is Stephen King, but you cannot bring yourself to offer up his books . . .

> try harder.

If a teen boy wants sports, and your first thought is Chris Crutcher . . .

> try Carl Deuker.

If your first thought was Gary Paulsen, but *Dogsong* was not exciting enough, try . . .

> Ben Mikaelsen. *Touching Spirit Bear.* HarperCollins, 2001.

If your first thought was Stephenie Meyer's *Twilight,* try . . .

> A. M. Jenkins. *Night Road.* HarperTeen, 2008.

If he likes cars more than reading, don't give up . . .

> try Todd Strasser's Drift X series.

If you even think about giving him Jean Craighead George's *Julie of the Wolves,* try . . .

> Graham Salisbury. *Night of the Howling Dogs.* Wendy Lamb, 2007.

If your first thought is John Green's *Looking for Alaska,* try . . .

> John Green. *An Abundance of Katherines.* Dutton, 2006.

If your first thought is Richard Adams's *Watership Down,* try . . .

> Kenneth Oppel. *Silverwing.* Simon and Schuster, 1997.

If your first thought is John Knowles's *A Separate Peace,* try . . .

> Joseph Bruchac. *Code Talker: A Novel about the Navajo Marines of World War Two.* Speak, 2005.

If your first thought is Joseph Conrad's *Heart of Darkness,* try . . .

> David Grann. *The Lost City of Z: A Tale of Deadly Obsession in the Amazon.* Doubleday, 2009.

CONCLUSION

I hope you have enjoyed this stroll through the world of readers' advisory for boys. Yes, I hope it was useful, challenging, and inspiring as well, but do not overlook the importance of pure enjoyment. Ultimately, the goal of readers' advisory for boys is not to make them read books, but to turn boys into readers. That will require them to enjoy reading, or they will read only when they are forced to. Being a reader means having the habit of reading, making it an integral—and integrated—part of your life. It is surpassingly sad that this does not describe many boys' experiences with reading. We worry that boys who drop out of school before they develop the habit are doomed to lives as nonreaders, but I have met too many boys who look forward to high school graduation as the day when they no longer have to read.

Why do we need to consider gender in readers' advisory? Because boys and girls are different. Not all boys fit any kind of mold, but enough of them share traits—traits often concurrent with reading problems—that we must pay attention. Nothing in this book is meant to be proscriptive. Everything is designed to make you think. If you are having trouble reaching a boy, there are any number of issues included here that might explain the problem, and just as many approaches that may be employed to fix it. Here, at the very end, let me reiterate the overriding message of this work, and my twenty years of trying to connect boys and reading.

Readers' advisory is about creating readers, and that requires addressing the whole child. It is not enough to put a book in a boy's hands. There are so many factors that discourage a boy from reading, starting with the perceptions he is likely to have before you even encounter him. His society does not give him examples of men reading; his family may not as well. We honor the male in athletics, in business, in entertainment, but not in education. Too many men in this society hide when they read. The vast majority of the adults that boys see read are female.

Supporting that perception of reading as a feminine activity is the apparent failure of males when it comes to reading. We judge readers based on their age, not their developmental stage, and we create standards that say this is the appropriate level of skill in reading you should have. We ignore the fact that skill comes from reading, not the other way around. Because of that, we push kids to read at some artificial level of proficiency and stress them out when they fail to meet that level. That stress hangs above the heads of many boy readers you encounter every day. This makes boys feel disconnected from reading. It is an external hurdle they must clear, nothing more.

Adding to the level of disconnect is the fact that we define what is good literature, real reading, and appropriate books, all without reference to the types of reading that speak to boys. Why should a boy listen to you when you are just another adult pushing books on him that do not touch his life? Whether you are in fact guilty of such crimes or not, all that background informs the readers' advisory experience.

And although all these factors put up barriers to your effective readers' advisory, there are simple facts of distance that mean you may never have the chance to reach out to boys. They are often not in the library where you are, when you are. They are on the basketball court, online, in class, anywhere that their busy lives take them. If they feel disconnected from reading, entering the book shrine is not going to be high on their priority list.

You must address all these factors to be effective at readers' advisory. A boy's psychology, family, social setting, schedule, prejudices, and stress level are as important as his reading level when it comes to putting the right book in his hand. On one side, you have all these disparate factors, and a thousand more, all funneling down to the shaggy-haired boy holding a skateboard in front of you. On the other side, you have an endless world of reading choices, many more than we generally consider, branching out to a horizon of possibilities you cannot see. Where do these two eternities meet? In the present, and in you. I told you back in the beginning not to panic, but do not lose sight of the enormity of the work you do either. You are at the center of an hourglass, with all the grains that make up a boy's experience coming together at a vital point, and all the empty space of possibilities waiting beyond.

Acknowledge the whole boy, all that made him what he is, and help him to see all that lies before him as a reader. That is so much more than handing him a book.

BIBLIOGRAPHY

Abilock, Debbie. "Sex in the Library: How Gender Differences Should Affect Practices and Programs." *Emergency Librarian* (May/June 1997): 17.

Ashby, Susan. "Reading Doesn't Have to Damage Your Street Cred." *Youth Studies Australia* (March 1998): 46.

Bloom, Adi. "Girls Go for Little Women but Boys Prefer Lara." *Times Educational Supplement* (March 15, 2002): 18.

Doiron, Ray. "Boy Books, Girl Books." *Teacher Librarian* (February 2003): 14–16.

Elias, Marilyn. "Electronic World Swallows Up Kids' Time, Study Finds." *USA Today* (March 10, 2005): A1.

Fine, Jon. "Where the Boys Aren't." *BusinessWeek* (November 7, 2005): 24.

Hannaford, Carla. *Smart Moves: Why Learning Is Not All in Your Head.* Arlington, VA: Great Ocean Publishers, 1995.

Ingles, Steven J., et al. *A Profile of the American Sophomore in 2002: Initial Results from the Base Year of the Education Longitudinal Study of 2002.* Washington, DC: National Center for Education Statistics, 2005.

Jones, Patrick, and Dawn Cartwright Fiorelli. "Overcoming the Obstacle Course: Teenage Boys and Reading." *Teacher Librarian* (February 2003): 9.

Keane, Nancy J., and Terence W. Cavanaugh. *The Tech-Savvy Booktalker: A Guide for 21st-Century Educators.* Westport, CT: Libraries Unlimited, 2009.

Langerman, Deborah. "Books and Boys: Gender Preferences and Book Selection." *School Library Journal* (March 1990): 132–36.

Nielsen, Alleen Pace. "It's Deja Vu All Over Again!" *School Library Journal* (March 2001): 49–50.

Pirie, B. *Teenage Boys and High School English.* Portsmouth, NH: Heinemann, 2002.

Pomerantz, Eva M., Ellen Rydell Altermatt, and Jill L. Saxon. "Making the Grade but Feeling Distressed: Gender Differences in Academic Performance and Internal Distress." *Journal of Educational Psychology* (June 2002): 396.

Pottorff, Donald D., Deborah Phelps-Zientarski, and Michelle E. Skovera. "Gender Perceptions of Elementary and Middle School Students about Literacy at Home and School." *Journal of Research and Development in Education* (Summer 1996): 211.

Renwick, Lucille. "What's the Buzz?" *Instructor* (August 2001): 8.

Ripley, Amanda. "Who Says a Woman Can't Be Einstein?" *Time* (March 7, 2005): 55.

Sanford, Kathy, Heather Blair, and Raymond Chodzinski. "A Conversation about Boys and Literacy." *Teaching and Learning* (Spring 2007): 5.

Sommers, Christina Hoff. *The War against Boys.* New York: Simon and Schuster, 2000.

Taliaferro, Lanning, "Education Gender Gap Leaving Boys Behind." *Journal News* (June 17, 2001): 17.

Taylor, Donna Lester. "'Not Just Boring Stories': Reconsidering the Gender Gap for Boys." *Journal of Adolescent and Adult Literacy* (December/January, 2005): 290–98.

Turner, Thomas N. "Book Talks: Generating Interest in Good Reading." *Social Education* (May/June 2005): 195–99.

INDEX